Buckaroos in Paradise

Branding iron from the Circle A.

OVERLEAF:
The 96 Ranch herd arrives at the Hartscrabble line camp. Each fall the cattle are brought back to the valley in a three-day, thirty-mile drive.

Bob Humphrey, Clale Northrup, and John DeHaan watch the cattle they have gathered at the Cold Springs line camp during the 1978 fall roundup for the 96 Ranch. Cows and calves that were separated during the day "mother up" and become quiet for the night's rest and feeding.

Buckaroos in Paradise

Cowboy Life in Northern Nevada

HOWARD W. MARSHALL
American Folklife Center
Library of Congress

RICHARD E. AHLBORN
Division of Community Life
Smithsonian Institution

Publication for an Exhibition
at the
NATIONAL MUSEUM OF HISTORY AND TECHNOLOGY
Smithsonian Institution, Washington, D.C.
October 1, 1980—March 31, 1981

LIBRARY OF CONGRESS
WASHINGTON
1980

PUBLICATIONS OF THE AMERICAN FOLKLIFE CENTER; NO. 6

The publication of this book through the Elizabeth Hamer Kegan Fund of the Library of Congress was assisted by a generous donation from the Garvey Kansas Foundation, Wichita.

LIBRARY OF CONGRESS CATALOGING IN PUBLICATION DATA

Marshall, Howard W.
Buckaroos in Paradise.

"Exhibition catalogue": p.
Bibliography: p.
1. Cowboys—Nevada—Paradise Valley—Exhibitions. 2. Paradise Valley, Nev.—Social life and customs—Exhibitions. 3. Ranch life—Nevada—Paradise Valley—Exhibitions. I. Ahlborn, Richard E., joint author. II. National Museum of History and Technology. III. Title.
F847.H8M37 979.3'54 80-23261
ISBN 0-8444-0348-2

COVER:
Dan Martinez at a spring branding near one of the Circle A line camps.

ENDPAPERS:
Brands from some Paradise Valley ranches.

Contents

Homer Ely at a spring branding on the 96 Ranch.

Foreword

The exhibition "Buckaroos in Paradise," together with this publication, presents the artifacts of a particular way of life in a particular place in the western United States. Paradise Valley, Nevada, is to a certain extent emblematic of the larger Great Basin region and the American West generally. Regional presentations such as "Buckaroos in Paradise," as they sharpen our focus on specific sections of the Western landscape, inevitably raise new perplexities about the nature and definition of cultural regions and subregions of the country. Such perplexities are welcome, since they result from a desire to be more precise and attentive to detail in our explorations of the nation's regional diversity.

If the geographical significance of "Buckaroos in Paradise" is complex, its historical meaning is even more mystifying. Most of us justify our interest in history by saying that it relates to the present, but we tend to think of it in segmented chronological periods separated from each other and from the present day. "Past" in our minds is all too easily cut off from "present," almost as if such distinctions were our only means of focusing on the bewildering continuum of human existence.

Thus the present exhibition may prove perplexing to some. Does it show how things used to be in Paradise Valley or how things are today? Is it a balanced sampling of typical objects and activities? Is it weighted toward the old-fashioned? Does it emphasize the locally produced and the handcrafted rather than the mass-produced artifacts of popular culture? Is it simply a picture of everyday life, or does it put a premium on the artful expression of that life? All these questions express a tension that informs this exhibition and publication—a tension expressed by professional folklorists in a term which has become for them a keyword, *tradition*. It is tradition which embraces those contradictory poles, making bedfellows of past and present, ordinary and expressive, in the cultural view presented in "Buckaroos in Paradise."

ALAN JABBOUR
Director, American Folklife Center

Preface

The exhibition "Buckaroos in Paradise" at the National Museum of History and Technology is a sampling of artifacts and images from the daily lives of Great Basin buckaroos in the contemporary West. It signals a return of national interest in the West and typifies the growing interest in recording and studying the complex traditional cultural landscapes around us.

The objects and the information result from the intensive study of a whole community—Paradise Valley, Nevada—in which the working cowboy (called "buckaroo" by insiders) is but one feature. The Paradise Valley Folklife Project, conducted by the American Folklife Center in the Library of Congress, documented a wide range of cultural expression, from cooking to coyote trapping to immigration history, but the buckaroo and his vital role on the family and corporation ranches provided a continual focus.

"Buckaroos in Paradise" is a celebration of a way of life and of the artifacts that empower and vivify the "cowboy trade" and the West. The artifacts are both historical and contemporary, things built, used, consumed, and discarded in everyday life by cowboys and ranch families.

There is a general agreement about what we mean when we say "the West." This large, complicated West of common parlance begins at about the ninety-eighth meridian, knifing down from Canada through the Dakotas, Nebraska, Kansas, Oklahoma, and through Texas to Mexico. There are places where the land seems to say "welcome to the West"—at about Salina, Kansas, for example, between St. Louis and Denver. Although regional character and climate differ, this enormous West has been developed over one-hundred fifty years by fur traders' expeditions, settlement, Manifest Destiny, mining and railroad booms, United States Geological Survey parties, cattle ranching, Las Vegas, and Environmental Impact Statements. It is on this broad canvas that communities glow with a particularly western light. Just as our misinformed stereotypes and preconceptions of other American regions are corrected by a thoughtful visit, our picture of the West is surely redrawn when there is time to listen, observe, and record the words and the view accurately.

What can we do for the people we visit? For some people in Para-

Leslie Stewart

Marie Stewart

dise Valley, we have already done it: by visiting them and documenting their way of life and work, we have effectively put them into the formal record of American civilization. Beyond the present products of our work—an exhibition and some publications—the information and artifacts have become part of the permanent collections of the Library of Congress and the Smithsonian Institution, for use and study by the present and future generations. Future research and writing on that part of the West must take account of the record of Paradise Valley and northern Nevada. Our visits and research would have been impossible without the hospitality and consideration shown us by many individuals and families in the region. Our relationships with people in Nevada make the usual scholar's term "informant" inappropriate if not downright untenable. We became attached to the place and we would like to think of ourselves as friends.

There are important changes in the life of the buckaroo—agricultural technology, livestock transportation, the four-wheel-drive truck, the gradual lessening of the need to stay out "on the mountain" in buckaroo camps, the spread of real farming—but for the most part the range cattle industry, a peculiarly Western American economic system, is much the same as it was fifty years ago. In its social order and its essential vision of how life and work should be, the buckaroo's world is as it was when the first Anglo and California Mexican vaqueros moved and worked cattle for the large family ranchers and—even earlier—for corporation outfits like Abel and Curtner or Miller and Lux. The itinerant, shifting labor force that did much of the seasonal "grub" work—buckaroos—is still necessary even though the small family ranch is endangered by the modern world.

This exhibition is an impression of one Western valley and way of life today. But its story of immigration, settlement, development of the range cattle industry, and success today is the story not just of these buckaroos and ranching families but of the American West that is in some ways still our favorite frontier.

In the Paradise Valley project, which spanned more than two years, teams of field researchers representing different academic approaches documented various aspects of traditional life. Out of the seasonal research activities, each team member was asked to produce fieldnotes, logs to tape recordings and photographs, and a manuscript on a selected topic important in the region's cultural history and personality today. On the team, I was responsible for directing the project and for work in material culture and family history. Carl Fleischhauer of the American Folklife Center served as media specialist and worked with William Smock to produce the film of the 96 Ranch round-up and trail drive that accompanies the exhibition. Richard E. Ahlborn, curator of community life at the Smithsonian's National Museum of History and Technology, joined us to document

Geraldine and Joe Boggio

Fred Miller

Robert Cassinelli

Walter Fischer

Ann Miller, with a picture of her parents

Alvin Miller and Wesley Faupel

Delfina Zatica

Pete Pedroli

Marguerite Faupel

ranch crafts and horsegear and served as the curator of the exhibition. Keith Cunningham, a professor of folklore at Northern Arizona University, documented oral traditions concerning the town of Paradise Valley. James Deetz, director of the Lowie Museum at the University of California, Berkeley, led a team of historical archaeologists (Eugene Prince, Lynn Eisenmann, and Jamey Deetz) in a survey of the historic Chinese community near the town. Linda Gastañaga, a Basque studies specialist in Reno who has family ties in the valley, studied the Basque presence. Suzi Jones, an Oregon folklorist now in Alaska, studied material culture. William Smock, an ethnographic photographer and filmmaker with Pictures and Words, San Francisco, co-produced the 96 Ranch film for the exhibition and photographed a variety of activities on other visits. Thomas Vennum, an ethnomusicologist with the Smithsonian's Folklife Programs, studied Paiute Indians as ranch hands and buckaroos. William A. Wilson, a folklore professor at Utah State University, documented the yearly round on several of the family ranches.

Most importantly, the exhibition owes its existence to the hospitality and kindness of people in Humboldt County, Nevada, and Dick Ahlborn and I wish to thank them. Those who saw the importance of the exhibition and gave, sold, or lent their possessions so it could be achieved are Joe and Geraldine Boggio, Bob Cassinelli, Marguerite Faupel, Wesley Faupel, Walter and Irene Fischer, Alvin and Ann Miller, Fred Miller, Pete Pedroli, Leslie and Marie Stewart, and Delfina Zatica. Other artifacts were lent from various divisions of the National Museum of History and Technology. Many other people helped us understand the buckaroo life, and in addition to those named above, this publication is dedicated to Theodore Brown, the Buckinghams, the Cerris, Harold Chapin, the DeHaans, Dick Gusky, Dave Hiller, Frank Loveland, Ernest and Emily Miller, the Northrups, Herb Pembroke, the Recanzones, the Schwartzes, the Felix Scott family, Fred Stewart, the Taylors, and Chuck and Lola Wheelock.

Alan Jabbour, director of the American Folklife Center, and Roger Kennedy, director of the National Museum of History and Technology, encouraged and supported the exhibition's development. Deborah M. Bretzfelder designed the exhibition at the museum. This publication would not have been possible without the generous assistance of the Garvey Kansas Foundation and the support of Willard and Jean Garvey, who know Paradise Valley and buckaroo life.

Howard W. Marshall

Buckaroos in Paradise

At the Circle A Little Owyhee line camp.

Buckaroo: Views of a Western Way of Life

HOWARD W. MARSHALL

The Cowman's Dominion

The broad region that encloses Nevada is variously called the Intermountain West, the Basin and Range Province, and the Intermountain Sagebrush Province. It includes southeastern Oregon, southern Idaho, southwestern Wyoming, western Colorado, Utah, Nevada, and California's eastern slope. During his second long exploration of 1842-43, John C. Frémont called this massive continental trough spreading from the Rockies to the Sierras "the Great Basin," its most common name today. For a long time the region was called the Great American Desert. Everyone from Horace Greeley to the young Mark Twain to traveler-writers like Samuel Bowles joked about its desolate barrenness.

The region northern Nevada more particularly shares and represents includes southeastern Oregon, a piece of southwestern Idaho, and northeastern California. In this big heart of the Great Basin, both the land and the work define a cultural region with a special personality. It is chiefly the territory of the range cattle industry now, and settlement is mostly confined to clusters of ranches, ranching communities, and small cities spaced along Interstate Highway 80, where county governments function and the gaming and entertainment business thrives. Interstate 80, the modern superhighway, follows safely along the old emigrant trail, the Humboldt River, and at times the Southern Pacific Railroad mainline. It is a land of great distances, great panoramas, and great cattle ranches.

The Mill Ranch, Paradise Valley, and the Santa Rosa Mountains.

This huge Intermountain West comprises vacant, semiarid deserts and mountain ranges that rise up out of the distance like ghosts. It both frightened and lured the emigrants passing through on the California trails in the mid-nineteenth century. The great Humboldt River, the pioneer's lifeline, is unlike others that empty into the Gulf of Mexico or the Pacific Ocean: it rises in the mountains and disappears in the desert.

The state of Nevada has a small population, and the majority of people live in the two main cities, Reno and Las Vegas. Only one United States representative is elected to serve in the House. Nevada's state flower is the sagebrush. Its state tree is the piñon pine, and the state bird is the mountain bluebird. It is the fifth largest state in size and nearly the smallest in population. With about four inches of rainfall a year, it is the driest. Federal agencies own and manage 87 percent of all the land in Nevada, as they control 54 percent of the entire Western United States.

Paradise Valley, the focus of the project and the exhibition, is about forty miles long and twelve miles wide. "Shelton lane" divides the "upper end" or "upper valley" from the "lower end" or "lower valley." The valley is walled in on the west and north by the 9,000-foot peaks of the Santa Rosa Range, where pine and quaking aspen grow, and on the southeast by the lower Hot Springs Range. The lower end opens out around the Little Humboldt River, where Martin Creek and Cottonwood Creek join it, and spreads into the sagebrush flats south toward Winnemucca, the county seat and business center of Humboldt County. Paradise Valley, at 4,600 feet, is cattle and hay country with scarce water and a growing season of about ninety days. Its modern capacity

Black Ridge line camp, 96 Ranch.

to produce fine crops and cows is largely the result of intricate and efficient irrigation systems that pioneer farmers and ranchers checkered across the cleared fields. The region is at once inviting and threatening. With only seven to nine inches of rain each year, the people depend on the winter's snowfall and snowpack in the mountains, which produces the spring runoff that renews the bunchgrass, brings back creeks, and provides water for the irrigation of pastures and fields that sustain cattle herds through the following winter.

The summers are very hot but the winters are moderate. Spring comes early, and there is almost no summer rain. There are few permanent streams, and occasional dry years slow to a trickle even steady creeks like Martin and Cottonwood. It is a world of sagebrush, alkali flats, bare gray mountains, and stark beauty. Just over the valley's eastern apron lies the vast Owyhee Desert, where no farming has succeeded. The endless sagebrush and rocky hills are broken only by an occasional buckaroo camp nestled in a draw or canyon. Thin lines of aspens and willows in these places enfold the small creeks flowing on into the Owyhee and Little Humboldt rivers.

Emigrants, Miners, Railroads, Ranchers

The area that became Nevada was only sparsely settled when the region of Upper California was given over to the United States by the "Mexican Cession" (Treaty of Guadalupe Hidalgo) in 1848. It had barely been explored. Gold and silver ore still lay undisturbed by pickaxes and black powder gangs.

A band of sheep in the town of Paradise Valley. According to local historian Fritz Buckingham, the picture was taken during the 1920s and shows Jose Gastañaga with the valley's last band of sheep.

By the time Nevada became an official territory in 1861 (after separation from the Utah Territory), the Comstock Lode had been developed and the new territorial seal sported a mining scene. By the time of statehood in 1864 the cattle industry and buckaroo trade were just starting up and had attained no particular influence or character. The 1864 state seal again showed hardock mining but added a steam locomotive and a railroad trestle. Still, many a teamster and miner saw that there was a better and more permanent life to be had in selling cattle to miners than in *being* miners.

Following the big mining years, the bonanza generation of ranchers and businessmen like Angelo Forgnone, Aaron Denio, William Stock, and Charles Kemler saw the opening of the region by the Central Pacific Railroad, which reached Winnemucca in 1868 and built yards and shops there. The budding town was originally called French Ford, after the river crossing and village started by a French fur trader, and was renamed in honor of the peaceful and influential Paiute chief when the transcontinental railroad's western division passed through on its way to completion in northern Utah a year later.

Humboldt County borders Oregon on the north and Idaho on the northeast. It fills a space the size of some eastern states, yet its population is about seven thousand. Winnemucca, a small city, grew up around the Humboldt River crossing and like other towns got its big push when the railroad worked its way by. The railroad made Winnemucca important as a shipping point, and it soon replaced the larger mining town of Unionville as the county's hub. In the 1870s Winnemucca bloomed as a railhead for cattle driven

MC CONNELL PEAK
7531
EIGHTMILE MOUNTAIN
7853
Klondike Canyon
National Mine
CAPITOL PEAK
8255
LONG CANYON
5797
6148
Ranch
5626
Halcyon Mine
BUCKSKIN MOUNTAIN
8743
Goosey Lake Flat
QUINN RIVER VALLEY
SANTA ROSA RANGE
Water
4358
GRANITE PEAK
9732
Martin Creek Ranger Station
HINKEY SUMMIT
8554
Cabin
Coons Flat
Charlie Young Can
Corral
6054
7128
HUMBOLDT NATIONAL FOREST
Spring Canyon
Orovada
4212
SANTA ROSA PEAK
9701
SUGAR LOAF HILL
6697
5743
Paradise Valley Ranger Substation
Ranches
5824
6128
6194
Horse Canyon
PARADISE PEAK
9443
Paradise Valley
4500
Buffalo Canyon
5982
4713
4R Ranch
4460
4544
TRAP BUTTE
4468
8669
4208
HOT SPRINGS PEAK
6450
Sonoma Mine
Plant
7218
4571
5152
SILVER STATE VALLEY
BLOODY RUN HILLS
Davetown
4217
Windmill
4375
PARADISE VALLEY
HOT SPRINGS RANGE
Stewart Gap
EDEN VALLEY
4950
4629
4704
4336
6556
Anderson Canyon
6837
Burn Canyon
Soldier Cap
Getchell Mine
1
2
3
4
5
6
7
8
9
10
11
12
13
14
15
16
17
18
19
20
21

PARADISE VALLEY
Humboldt County, Nevada

1. Bradshaw line camp (96 Ranch)
2. Cold Spring line camp (96 Ranch)
3. Black Ridge line camp (96 Ranch)
4. Little Owyhee line camp
5. Hartscrabble line camp (96 Ranch)
6. Site of Ft. Winfield Scott
7. Schwartz Ranch
8. Recanzone's Home Ranch
9. Boggio's 7 U P Ranch
10. Town of Paradise Valley
11. Bradshaw-Cerri-Wallace Ranch
12. Cassinelli's Mill Ranch
13. Singas Creek Ranch
14. Stewart's 96 Ranch
15. Ferraro Ranch
16. Fred Miller Ranch
17. Shelton Lane
18. Paradise Hill
19. Miller's 101 Ranch
20. Taylor's Triple T Ranch
21. To Winnemucca

Detail from a map prepared by the U.S. Army Topographic Command 1956.
Revised by the U.S. Geological Survey 1971.

to the loading pens from across northern Nevada and the "Owyhee country" in southeastern Oregon and southern Idaho. The Central Pacific hauled most of the market cattle west toward the Sacramento Valley and San Francisco slaughterhouses, although some were shipped to the Midwest.

Since it had no railroad shipping point or continual industry (the mines flourished only briefly), the town of Paradise Valley established itself as a community to service and be served by family and corporation ranches. But it was no "cow town" of the sort we are accustomed to seeing in popular images. It reached a population peak around the turn of the century, when the sheep business brought more Basque herders than buckaroos to the valley. Winnemucca was the county seat, railhead, and center of commercial enterprises, and Paradise Valley, with a current population of about two hundred and fifty, still has a satellite character. The town is at the end of Nevada State Road 8B that branches northeast off U.S. 95 at Paradise Hill between Winnemucca and the Oregon state line at McDermitt. Although the valley seems tucked off in the mountains, it was never and is not now isolated from business, communication, and transportation centers. It is forty miles from Winnemucca but never was cut off from ties to the county seat and the rest of the nation. By the time Paradise Valley was effectively settled and the cattle industry was blooming in the 1870s, the little town was thriving, with constant goings and comings from other regions, chiefly Oregon and the Sacramento Valley and northern California. Ties with Sacramento have always been very strong, and families maintain the old California connection. Most of the first settlers came into northern Nevada from California. They imported everything from English ironstone china to the California Mexican vaqueros who put their lasting stamp on cattle-raising and horsegear traditions in the valley. They sent for catalogue furniture, Belgian draft horses, Hereford breeding stock, Portland cement, garden seeds, lombardy poplar saplings, blue denim work pants, Aladdin lamps, radios, Fords, Winchester rifles, and terra cotta chimney pots. For almost a century, families in Paradise Valley have sent not only their products to market in California but their children to Berkeley for high school as well.

Paradise City (renamed Paradise Valley by the 1870s) grew up around the ranch of C. A. Nichols (now the Boggio 7 U P Ranch), as newcomers in the

Paradise Valley's main street, about the turn of the century.

late 1860s began to locate their homesteads near Fort Winfield Scott, the short-lived U.S. Cavalry post in the upper end of the valley on Cottonwood Creek. Charles Kemler was the town's first big businessman and along with Alphonso Pasquale a chief developer in the early generation. Kemler's house was the first hotel, schoolhouse, and lodge hall. In its heyday the town had the usual assortment of wagonmaking shops, blacksmith shops, general stores, livery stables, hotels, and saloons. A white frame Methodist church (1893), now a community church, and a gray granite Catholic church face west on the town's main road. There is a volunteer fire department. Frank Meyers operated an adobe brick factory and put up nearly all the many adobe buildings in the valley. William Kirschner operated a lager beer brewery in the basement of his adobe house on Cottonwood Creek, and Italian families still go to California in the fall to bring back Zinfandel grapes for making wine on the ranches. The town's first lawyer and schoolteacher, J. B. Case (from Tennessee via California), went into storekeeping and hired Steve Boggio (one of the many north Italians in Paradise) to build a fine granite store in 1910 that now is Jerry Sans's bar. The Odd Fellows lodge was chartered in 1874, the Daughters of Rebekah in 1884, and for years the lodge hall has been the adobe store building that was once one of Charles Kemler's enterprises. The U.S. Forest Service came to town in 1935, and Civilian Conservation Corps crews built their headquarters, the town's grammar school, and other structures around the valley. The "C C boys" built the road up over Hinkey Summit out of the valley to the northwest, and laid the state road branch from Paradise Hill in 1938, making obsolete the old wagon road that went straight down to Winnemucca.

High school students today ride the bus to Winnemucca's Lowry High, a trip taking a good hour and a half each way. The town is changing again, as full-time farming increases in popularity and as more people find it a good place to settle in their retirement, to establish summer homes, or to commute to

Winnemucca from. Ernest and Emily Miller, who ran Case's Store for many years, keep the town's post office open, although the town's population is a few hundred and the operation is only marginally profitable. The "mail stage" from Winnemucca pulls in at Miller's post office at 10:00 every morning of the week, and valley people have a chance to exchange news and conversation when they come to fetch mail from their boxes. Buckaroos drive to town to check mail and sometimes stop in at Jerry Sans's bar for a moment of relaxation and a break in the monotony of the work. On most mornings, a cast of regulars drink coffee and trade stories in Frank Gavica's garage behind Sans's. Like the buckaroo trade which gives the town its reason for existence, the pace of activity is generally slow.

Thompson and West's history of Nevada (republished by Myron Angel) described Paradise Valley in 1881.

> [*Paradise Valley*] *is one of the* oases *sometimes found in the most barren and desolate countries, like Broussa, in Syria, or the vale of Cashmere, in Persia. . . . As, from its fertility and favorable situation, it is likely to become the most important permanent agricultural portion of Nevada, an account of its discovery and settlement well deserves a place in the history of the State.*
>
> *About the first of June, 1863, R. D. Carr, W. B. Huff, J. A. Whitmore and W. C. Gregg started from Star City with the intention of prospecting the mountains on the north side of the Humboldt, ranging to the east. They crossed near where Mill City now stands, and followed the western slope of*

Paradise Valley, 1978.

Italian immigrant settlers Mr. and Mrs. John Forgnone at their ranch.

the mountains until they struck Rebel Creek, which they followed to its source near the summit. On attaining the summit a wide and beautiful valley burst on their view. Having seen only canyons and rugged hills they were much surprised, and W. B. Huff involuntarily exclaimed, "What a paradise!" and thus gave a name to the valley.

These prospectors saw the chance at hand, came back the following year to set up homesteads, and began growing crops and cattle. Indian raids in 1865 brought the Army post and further settlement, and by the time the post was closed in 1871 the valley was on its way. The place-name legend involving the prospectors has been kept in circulation in the community, and most people today have some version of the story of "how Paradise Valley got its name." It is a question we often asked in our field research. Like the variant dressed up and published by Thompson and West, current variants of the legend contain certain vital facts—that the valley was first found by

Illustration from Thompson and West's history of Nevada. For many years the William Stock Farming Company, this ranch is now called the "96."

prospecting hardrock miners and that they were surprised and thrilled at its beauty.

In March of 1978, Ernest Miller, a grandson of German pioneer Gerhard Miller, Sr., told me this variant, matter-of-factly:

> *They said that they, in the real old times, there was a couple prospectors came up from the valley on the west side of us and they come up on top of the beautiful Santa Rosa range, and when they looked over the top they said, "Now isn't this a beautiful paradise!"*

The story was told in a similar way in October 1979 by Butch Recanzone's wife Vicki, a Californian, who heard the place-name legend when she married and moved to the valley.

> *Well, the only story I ever heard was that someone came up over the Santa Rosas, and looked down into the valley after seeing nothing but sagebrush and desert and said that this* was *a paradise, because there was water down here and it was green and there were trees. And now* that's *what I heard. You know, that they looked down and saw a paradise. And being that it is a valley, there's no doubt about that.*

In any story-telling situation, others present chime in with enlargements, confirmations, additional information, or reflections. Here Vicki's father-in-law Carlo Recanzone added: "But I know that they've always said that they came from the north. And came across the Santa Rosas, and looked down upon this thing, and says, 'Oh, this is paradise.' [laughter] So, that's the way they say the name came."

The people who settled the valley have names like Bradshaw, Harvey, Byrnes, Case, Lye, and Shelton, but also names like Ferraro, Stock, Schwartz, Recanzone, Kemler, Pasquale, and Forgnone. Historian Wilbur Shepperson shows that within several years after statehood Nevada was peopled by immigrants from nearly forty foreign countries and five continents. Yet in this huge state of more than a dozen mountain ranges, certain groups settled in certain places. In Paradise Valley, the chief influx was from Germany, Italy, and the Basque provinces of France and Spain. Americans from the East, Midwest, and California joined these distinctive groups, as did English, Irish, French, and Swiss Italians. Others who appeared in the early days but failed to establish permanent settlements included Mexican vaqueros from California and a small community of Chinese.

No one group could claim to be the first settlers here. In spite of generations of acculturation and change, some ranchers and buckaroos are still most assuredly Italian or German. The three main groups of families—from other American places, from Italy, and from Germany—all came most immediately from northern California. The Germans came to farm and raise cattle and build commerce. The Italians came to ply their ancient craft as stonemasons and soon became ranchers and businessmen. The Basques, brought from California by Italians to tend sheep, became businessmen and ranchers themselves. The Basques had not been sheepherders before coming to Nevada; they worked in various occupations and many were gold and silver miners down on their luck. By the time the Basques were working into sheep and cattle ranching in the 1870s, there was a small Chinese neighborhood in Winnemucca made up of Chinese who stayed after serving as laborers building the Central Pacific Railroad along the Humboldt River past the town. Further, Paiute and Shoshone Indian men and women worked on ranches as buckaroos, hands, and cooks. The ethnic and linguistic mix must have been puzzling and bothersome to some pioneers. A businessman and rancher like Alphonso Pasquale, who operated a number of businesses in Paradise Valley and several sheep and cattle ranches in the valley, needed some fluency in six languages—his own Italian, English, German, French Basque, Spanish Basque, and Spanish—as well as a passing ability to make himself understood to Indian and Chinese employees.

Vaqueros

In the Great Basin range cattle industry, the vaqueros came first—not Anglo or black cowboys, but Hispanic California horsemen. In the Spanish colonial days before the cattle business developed, vaqueros worked mostly for hide and tallow companies in California. Later, as Anglo ranches and herds were being built up, the European-American pioneers employed Mexican vaqueros, and the vaquero traditions of horsemanship, equipment, and language greatly influenced other working cowboys. By the time the open-range cattle business reached its heyday in the generation after the Civil War and family and corporate ranches were thriving in northern Nevada, *vaquero* was the word used for *cowboy*. The legacy of expertise imparted by the oldtime vaqueros lives on in Paradise Valley, in the riatas and horsegear made by traditional "rawhiders" like Frank Loveland and the everyday use of Hispanic California-style, center-fired saddles with "taps" covering the stirrups.

Vaqueros were probably not a year-round fixture of the local scene in the early days in northern Nevada. They drove herds into the territory, providing breeding stock for ranchers, but the earliest farmer-ranchers did not or could not use many hired riders. Families helped neighboring families with cooperative labors, and the community's different herds of cattle "ran in common" on the open range. The first full-time, wage-earning vaqueros were probably employed by the big companies that for different reasons bought out small ranches in the county, slowly acquiring title or control of huge tracts and many small ranches that became "headquarters," foreman's homes, or buckaroo camps. Outfits like the Milpitas Land and Live Stock Company (with holdings in California, Nevada, and Idaho), Miller and Lux, and the butchering firm of Godchaux and Brandenstine (with headquarters in the San Francisco area), typified the large corporations that were influential alongside the family ranches in Nevada's growth. In time, the absentee-owned companies of the early days and later locally run corporations like the McCleary Cattle Company were bought out by corporations like today's Nevada Garvey Ranches, Inc., with head offices in Wichita, Kansas.

Vaqueros who began the buckaroo trade in the old Spanish times began the trade in Nevada, too, as the essential core of working men employed by the big companies. As these itinerant vaqueros from California and northern Mexico got acquainted in Nevada, they gradually became employees of local family ranches and remained in the region. Many of the early vaqueros were Anglos, of course, and several were black men.

Along with the rotating, changing population of wage-earning vaqueros who gradually became semi-

Myron Smart, a Paiute Indian buckaroo, on the 96 Ranch.

permanent in Paradise Valley, the pioneer family ranchers solved the problem of locating hired hands in a way that by the late nineteenth century had become a venerable American custom. They wrote letters home—whether to Illinois or Italy or Germany—and invited cousins, nephews, and brothers to come join them. Many young men got their start working for wages for a family member, gradually learning the business, saving up money, and then putting a payment down on a small spread of their own. Some of the young men "sold their saddles" and went into some sort of business enterprise.

In this essay, the three terms *vaquero, buckaroo,* and *cowboy* mean roughly the same thing. The term of preference in the early days in northern Nevada was *vaquero,* and the preferred word today is *buckaroo.* The term *cowboy* has never been used much in northern Nevada, where "cowboys" are from Texas, Montana, or some other place. Some scholars believe *buckaroo* comes from *bukra* (boss or white man) in the Gullah dialect of the Georgia and Carolina Sea Islands, and that the word was carried west and introduced into the cowboy's lexicon by black cowboys in Texas in the mid-nineteenth century. In northern

Dave Hiller files the bottom of a hoof flat before nailing a new shoe on a horse at the Circle A Little Owyhee line camp.

Nevada, though, our research supports a Spanish derivation for the etymology of *buckaroo*. *Vaquero* (from the Spanish *vaca* for *cow*) is the obvious source for *buckaroo*, and the oral testimony of ranchers adds significantly to the understanding of how *buckaroo* was Anglicized from *vaquero*. Reinforcing conversations at his ranch over two years' time, Leslie Stewart (grandson of William Stock, the German who developed the 96 Ranch) wrote me a letter in February 1980 summarizing his own experience this way:

> *The word "Buckaroo" sprang from the Spanish word "Vaquero," as you know "V" is pronounced "B." Even in the time I can remember the word Vaquero was used much more than Buckaroo, finally it was corrupted to Buckaroo. The word was not brought in by any specific group of early settlers as the Spanish word originated many, many years before this country was settled. The early Spanish Grant owners in California used the word for their herdsmen and horsemen in the time of the first settling of California and when it was still owned by Mexico. . . .*
>
> *The Spanish style and custom of working cattle spread into Nevada, Oregon and Idaho. Hence the Vaqueros or Buckaroos came with them. Even in this area in early days a large percentage of the riders were Mexicans or California Mexicans, especially on the larger outfits. One of my early, and fondest memories, is of the Circle A round-up crew annually coming up through our meadows on the way to the fall round-up. They had a Chuck Wagon drawn by six mules, a "Caviada" of many horses and 8 or more Mexican riders. They would generally stop here to get some eggs, potatoes, any other fresh garden produce that might be available and especially as much fresh homemade bread that my Mother might have for them.*

Stewart remembers a period in his youth, around 1935, when *buckaroo* became more popular in Nevada than *vaquero*, and today *buckaroo* is the word of daily use. The use of *buckaroo* by a cowboy, like the style of hat he wears and the kind of saddle he prefers, is a sign of origins and traditions. Knowledge and use of *buckaroo* separates insiders from outsiders.

Community language functions in different ways, from simply getting work done to providing insiders with a sense of identity and pride. The buckaroo's lexicon is distinguished by its deep bilingualism. Hispanic California vaqueros provided not only the way of work but the words of the trade. *Oreanna*, corresponding to *maverick* elsewhere, is the term for an unbranded cow running loose in Nevada; in earlier times a rancher could get started in the business by collecting oreannas and branding them. A buckaroo's long rope of braided rawhide used for catching animals is called a *riata* in northern Nevada; *lariat* is more familiar to other Americans.

Other terms of Spanish origin in northern Nevada, some of which are also used outside the Great Basin, include *bosal* (a small hackamore), *canyon, chapparal* (tough, thick brush), *caviata* or *cavvy* (the group of saddle horses used during roundup as the pool of mounts for buckaroos, called *remuda* elsewhere; each rider is assigned several specific horses which make up his "string"), *corral, chaps* (protective leather leg coverings of various styles; Nevadans prefer the short "chinks" variety or the "shotgun" variety), *dally* (as opposed to the "hard-and-fast" or "solid" roping style, the dally method loops the long riata or rope around the saddle horn so it can run or hold tight when a roped cow is being caught and held), *'dobe* (a building of local adobe bricks), *fiador* (or "theodore," a device consisting of a halter or a hackamore and a rope, knotted to the *romal*, that forms both a lead and a pair of closed reins), *hackamore* (a headstall or a halter for a horse, usually made of braided rawhide), *macardy* (long rope of twisted horsehair pulled from the mane or tail), *mustang* (wild horse), *savvy* (to comprehend another person's statement), and *taps* or *tapaderas* (leather covers or hoods over the stirrups). Many Anglo buckaroos command a working conversational ability in Spanish. Spanish words, and phrases like "mucho caliente!," pepper everyday speech. But the vaqueros themselves are almost completely absent from the trade today.

Working

The buckaroo life has undergone many changes since its nineteenth-century beginnings. Yet the object of attention is still the cows. Methods of working cattle and dealing with the land are learned by practice, by watching and listening to older hands, and by imitating and varying accepted models. The rules and standards, once learned, can be varied according to one's personal abilities and intentions. While buckaroos are individualists, they place a high value on the opinions and respect of their peers—and that respect must be earned. The basics of the business can be

96 Ranch buckaroo Homer Ely. Short chaps called "chinks" are worn during warm weather.

mastered in fairly short order—riding, using a rope correctly, baling hay during the summer, mending fence—but the many kinds of work range widely in difficulty. With practice, just about anyone can learn how to throw a rope to catch his horse in the morning or how to make a bedroll with some blankets and a big piece of heavy canvas. It takes more time and patience to learn to shoe horses, brand a cow without burning through the hide or making an uneven or upside-down mark, or wallow a truck out of a desert mudhole. Learning how to make reasonably good biscuits from scratch takes years of practice, and so does learning how to make a braided leather riata from a cow's hide. Most buckaroos master horseshoeing and branding; few buckaroos master biscuits or learn riata making.

There are different kinds of chores on a ranch. Dyed-in-the-wool cowboys prefer work on horseback. In the hierarchy of ranch employees there are bosses, buckaroos, ranch hands, and helpers. Below foreman or cow boss come buckaroos, expert horsemen at the center of the work. The special buckaroos who start colts (break horses)—often called "bronc busters" or "bronc peelers" — enjoy great respect if the job is skillfully and humanely done. Third in order are ranch hands and mechanics, who, though they also ride and help with herd work, are better at farming and equipment maintenance. A good mechanic is vital to the successful operation of a modern ranch, and a top one is harder to find than a top rider. Increasingly sophisticated and cranky haying equipment and machines, draped in grapevines of hydraulic lines, demand mechanical ability to keep them working right. Savvy in the shop is as important as savvy in the sagebrush, and the shaky state of the cow business makes the switch into full-time agriculture more socially acceptable for both employers and employees as time goes by. An "irrigator" is a ranch hand charged with properly managing and operating the agricultural watering system on the home ranch. Cooks and wranglers (who care for the horses) fall into this third group of men, too.

Harold Chapin

The fourth category, called helpers, includes young people who learn how to buckaroo, fix tractors, and run a ranch. It is a curious category, for it includes both green beginners and experienced oldtimers who may now want less strenuous assignments. Variously called helpers, swampers, choreboys, and hands, these workers need no particular special skills to accomplish the odd jobs that keep the ranch running smoothly—from bucking hay bales to swamping out the stables or painting a board fence around the garden. During the spring and fall periods of intense activity (calving, branding, round-up) and during the summer haying season, all employees join the labor of the moment. All the ranch employees can generally be called "ranch hands"—but seasoned buckaroos dislike being called that. A neat division of labor is practiced on the largest family ranches and the big corporation outfits where enough men are at work. On the small family ranch, however, everyone does everything, like it or not. The jobs you learn to do as a boy depend on who you are: if a young, would-be buckaroo with no particular roots or resources, you will likely learn horsemanship or machine-shop skills only, but if a rancher's son, you will likely learn everything possible. To grow into an effective ranch manager—a supervisor of experienced specialists—a young man must know every corner of the trade and the life. But first, he learns to buckaroo.

Carlo Recanzone started riding a horse at twelve and well remembers the oldtime buckaroos who taught him the profession. "They were real good teachers, but they were rough!" Boys of twelve would find it difficult to rise cheerfully before dawn, eat breakfast, go off in the chill mist, work, and return saddle-weary and hungry after dark. Every youngster comes to a moment that vividly marks the plateau when mastery of the skills is within sight. Many stories are told about losing cattle out in some canyon or desert draw; among the countless sins a boy or green hand could commit—from neglecting to keep closed gates closed and open gates open to jamming a hot iron on a cow sideways—the neglect or loss of cattle is very serious. A loss of a single cow can mean the loss of thousands of dollars, as well as wasted effort to locate the beast. A common mistake made by new or careless buckaroos is the needless hurrying along of walking cattle, and many a boy has been reprimanded for "chousing the cows."

Recanzone's son Butch, 30, has two words for how you learn to buckaroo: "Hard way." That is how young men have always gained proficiency in a trade or profession, whether as a cowboy or a stonemason, a sailor or a trial lawyer. As Butch Recanzone said in October 1979:

> *All it is is just another learnin' process. Trial and error. When you mess up you know about it, and the next time you don't do it. . . . You tried to pattern yourself after what they did.*

At a certain point, not at all mysterious, you make the grade. You know you have made it because the old hands stop calling you "boy." They start telling jokes *to* you instead of *about* you. You begin to be trusted to perform jobs on command and to conduct business professionally, and if you fail to get the work done right you soon become known as lazy or foolish. If you are a young man on a family ranch, you get a second chance. If you work for a corporation run by absentee owners, you might be asked to draw your pay, put your gear in your truck, and seek employment elsewhere.

Given an ordinary physique and a willingness to work, the essentials of skillful performance as a buckaroo boil down, as Les Stewart says, to a single ingredient: "judgment." Good judgment leads to the ability to be at "the right place at the right time" when riding and working. Mr. Stewart believes that good judgment, and the "right place at the right time" ability, make the difference between a good cowhand and simply a man mounted on a horse.

Cattlemen Were Farmers First

When William Stock, Batiste Recanzone, Jim Byrnes, the Lye brothers, and the other early settlers unloaded their wagons and set up homesteads in Paradise Valley, they were coming to be farmers and sheep growers as much as to be cowmen. The range cattle industry as we know it today was just beginning in the middle 1860s, and the Nevada settlers practiced agriculture as it was practiced across most of the West—as a diversified operation in which crops of grain were as important as cattle. Indeed, the first farmer-ranchers in northern Nevada started business in answer to the good markets for grain and hay and cattle in the booming mining centers like Virginia City and towns like Unionville. In the early phases of the business, families had their market crops freighted to the mining areas over wagon roads and largely sustained existence at home on what they could produce in their own gardens and farm lots. It took the coming of the railroad in the late 1860s to open up the ranching country and give the farmers and ranchers access to distant markets in California that soon became their chief commercial outlets.

The Old South is generally credited with the invention of the range cattle industry in the West, and perhaps rightly so, but in northern Nevada the business was developed by Midwesterners, Northerners, immigrants from Germany and Italy, and California Mexican vaqueros. The open-range cattle business glorified and exaggerated in popular fiction, movies, and television shows really flourished for a brief time, from about the end of the Civil War to about 1890. Because of a combination of economic conditions and the killing winters of the late 1880s, vast herds of

Feeding hay in March on the Taylors' Triple T Ranch.

Texas longhorns were no longer driven over thousands of miles of trails to Kansas or Missouri railheads and markets or to the frontier Northwest, and the cattle business settled into its modern character of family and corporation ranches raising cattle for local herd replenishment and regional markets. As Nevada settlers realized that scarce water supplies and low soil yield made the usual sort of farming operations difficult, they turned to a single enterprise for long-term investment, grazing cattle, mainly Hereford, on the open ranges. The names of the pioneering ranches reflect their initial goals and visions —like the William Stock Farming Company (1864), which today is a cattle ranch—and while they began to concentrate on cattle raising at the end of the nineteenth century, they continued to cultivate grains and hay crops for their own use and for local trade. Every Nevada rancher is a farmer too, since he must irrigate hayfields and harvest his own feed crops for feeding cattle through the winter on the home or "base" property. Few ranchers could afford to purchase winter feed, so they developed keen abilities and technical skills in the yearly cycle of irrigation and harvest of hay and grains.

In addition, many of the old cattle ranches began as sheep-raising operations. Particularly in the days

Robert Cassinelli turns water from the main irrigation ditch into a hayfield.

when cheap, good labor was available, before the federal grazing lands were enclosed and brought under control in the 1930s and before the development of synthetic fabrics, sheep were profitable. Ranches like the Stewarts' 96 (originally the William Stock Farming Company), the Recanzones' Home Ranch, the Millers' 101, and the Pasquale ranch owed at least part of their early success to the sheep industry. The 96 Ranch once ran as many as twelve thousand Merino sheep. For many of these farmer-ranchers, like the Stocks and Recanzones, the demise of the sheep trade was not exactly mourned. There were problems with landless "tramp herders" whose many sheep competed with local ranchers' cattle for scarce grass on the open range, and there was a gradual shift away from diversified stock toward concentration on range cattle. Some welcomed the sheep industry's end and turned their attention and resources to developing the cattle herds.

In Ernest Staples Osgood's treatment of the range cattle industry, the "range cattleman" is credited with certain contributions to the developing United States. He was the first to make effective economic use of the dry plains, and his business brought foreign investment to the economy, stimulated the national urge for building transcontinental railroads and communications networks, and laid the foundation for the development of communities and states in the region. To this list could be added the western rancher's refinement of irrigation processes. Domesticated crops were watered in systems of ditches by the Pueblo Indians in the American Southwest. Spanish colonization further refined irrigation techniques, and the Spanish colonial bureaucrats devised codes of water rights for farmers based on a tradition of prior use and first settlement. The techniques of watering crops in northern Nevada come out of Hispanic colonial usage, but they are also reminiscent of medieval British and European irrigation. Ranchers in the late nineteenth-century semiarid West brought irrigation to a fine science, and the old systems of banked ditches and headgates across fields remain effective today. At the same time, ranchers and farmers are taking advantage of new, complicated, and expensive water systems involving deep-drilled wells and sophisticated electric appliances and machines. The expanding cultivation of root crops, which need more water and fertilization than native strains of hay, ultimately means less natural annual moisture available for cattle and hayfields. As the annual snowfall, on which the ground-water yield in the valley is dependent, remains fairly steady over the years, use of deep wells and water technology will increase as the water table falls.

Family ranches have sizable gardens. In the early days, when more hired hands and larger families lived on the home ranch and when wives needed to can and preserve vegetables and fruits for home use, they were as large as 150 feet square. Today's best gardens are likely to be about 18 by 20 feet. They are laid out east to west and planted with some combination of cucumbers, tomatoes, lettuce, green beans, wax beans, onions, radishes, cabbage, carrots, beets, turnips, spinach, swiss chard, broccoli, peas, squash, and peppers. The perfectly ordered garden is framed by lilacs and other ornamental flowers and bushes. Ranchers long ago devised ingenious ways to water gardens by building an irrigation ditch from the nearest hayfield.

Ranching is a different operation in each particular region and climate. As Marion Clawson has written, it is the diversity of ranching that is striking, not the sameness. For the family rancher, and to a degree for the corporate outfits, the similarities are in the reliance on nature's ample or scarce resources in

Jesus Magaña breaks ground at the Cassinelli's Mill Ranch.

At the bar in Paradise Valley.

order to graze cattle or sheep for slaughter for human consumption; the need for sophisticated agricultural technology to support one's ranch competitively; the day-to-day engagement with a federal or state agency's regulations and regulators; the need for stout, quick cow horses to get certain jobs done; the carrying of huge debts to maintain yearly operation; the need for wage laborers during certain times of the year; and a liability to boom or bust according to the vicissitudes of national and international economic and political situations. In the West, there is a growing feeling among family ranchers that the control of their business and their future well-being is somehow vanishing. Some will survive while the unsupported or less capable will move off the land into Winnemucca, Reno, or San Francisco.

The Cowboy's Creed

Oh, when I die,
you just bury me
Away out west,
where the wind blows free.
Let cattle rub my tombstone down,
Let coyotes mourn their kin.
Let horses come and paw the mound,
But please, don't fence me in.

Tex Bonnet recited that poem for us in October 1979 in his white frame home on a quiet street in Winnemucca. It was a bright, clear fall day. Bonnet sat straight up in the chair, rested his hands on his knees, and stared ahead through the microphones. We had come to learn about the old buckaroo days and to record the stories, songs, and poems Bonnet knew so well and had become known for. You could tell he was thinking hard about the words as he spoke them. That serious bit of verse from a widely known poem that Bonnet had used over the years could serve as the buckaroo's creed.

The image of cowboys as ramblers and rugged individualists leading Teddy Roosevelt's "strenuous life," who shun the fences of civilization, indeed seems to hold up. They don't pack pistols, they don't croon mournful songs at cattle, they aren't uneducated. But to a man we found them purposeful individualists who cherish their work even while they complain about its inequities and problems. They would rather spend time making wages on horseback or in a line camp removed from town and regular society. These men volunteered for the job. As in any occupation, the laborers' complaints are thoroughly part of the life and the work itself.

"The cowboy" as a subject has been complicated by the national mythmaking process. The misinformation and stereotypes that trickled out of the West in travelers' reports and diatribes in the mid-nineteenth century turned into a flood in illustrated weeklies, dime novels, and wild west shows at century's end. Countless books, articles, radio programs, sound recordings, and Hollywood movies have kept up the flow of simplistic visions of the West. Occasionally movies or books appear presenting a more accurate view of buckaroos, but they make little popular headway. Not only is the image of the past distorted, but most people assume that there are no more buckaroos pushing cows through the bunchgrass.

Even in earlier days there was ample reading material available to cowboys, from the dime novel and *True West* through loftier literature. In Paradise Valley, buckaroos working in the cow camps do a great deal of reading. They read cattlemen's journals, outdoorsmen's magazines, *Reader's Digest*, and *Smithsonian;* popular paperback novels like *Rich Man, Poor Man* and *Oklahoma Crude;* and serious nonfiction like buckaroo Herb Pembroke's copy of a history of Russia and pocket editions of the classics. For many, the favorite topics are adventure, western themes, and the outdoor life, but for others something of Shakespeare is preferred. Certainly the particular heap of magazines and paperbacks on any line camp dinner table reflects haphazard selection and collection. Used books are exchanged by the batch at places in Winnemucca and purchased at the Poke and Peek Thrift Shop and the shop in the basement of the historical society museum.

Buckaroos live most of the year in some sort of house on the home ranch, but those who work for the big corporations spend weeks at a time out on the rangelands tending the cattle. They go to and from the camps in trucks, hauling horses, equipment, and supplies as they go. The buckaroo camps are without plumbing, electricity, or other luxuries of civilization. Working "on the mountain" and "on the wagon," many men like it that way. There is solitude, there is work, there is the land.

Many a long afternoon on the mountain (working cattle through the BLM or Forest Service grazing allotment) is spent in camp, when the day's work is done, and the hours are whittled away by an assortment of pastimes. Dave Hiller, a Nevada Vaca corporation cowboy in 1979, spent hours making horse gear from miscellaneous materials salvaged from the home ranch. The steel spurs he makes are not for the cases in the stores in town, but for his job. Bunkhouse furniture is homemade out of lumber highgraded from the ranch, and some buckaroos make their own riatas,

Tex Bonnet and folklorist Keith Cunningham.

macardies, and hackamores as well as lead ropes and other equipment. There is a great pride of workmanship in everything handmade, whether a piece of equipment is created from scratch or decorated to make it one's own.

There used to be a good deal of storytelling around evening cook fires, and sometimes a bit of singing or "music making," too. The stories generally were succinct accounts of scenes from life and history in the region, long personal anecdotes of memorable times, legends, or jokes. Storytelling sessions often commenced, then as now, with one man's offhand complaint or comment about one or another problem of the day. This gripe or thought leads to others on the same or different themes, which sometimes leads to testimonies and tales of how much better (or worse) things were in "the good old days." Cowboys as a group are very conscious of the real and imaginary history of their trade. Many a man has gone to the West and the buckaroo life in order to live legends. Although buckaroos and ranchers do not volunteer poems, "legends," or "folksongs," there are many such traditional forms of expression in circulation. Once in a while, usually in town, under the right combination of a late evening, good whiskey, juke box, and dancing partners, a fine poem or polished story will be recited about the castration of the mythical Strawberry Roan, or Butch Cassidy's legendary robbery of the First National Bank in Winnemucca. But these occasions are rare.

Buckaroo Dave Hiller with some horsegear he made at the Circle A Little Owyhee line camp.

Buckaroos own no land or house but do own personal property—a car or pickup truck, horsegear, household goods, a "war bag" of personal effects, bedroll, and other things that transport easily. Some own their own horses, which are kept and fed as though they were part of the rancher's cavvy. Working cowboys have a dwelling, wages, some groceries, and certain benefits according to the deal worked out—fresh beef butchered on the ranch, garden produce, access to the ranch gasoline pump, use of the machine shop, workmen's compensation, and other medical provisions. Most cowboys and other hired hands earn between five and six thousand dollars a year. Buckaroos working for wages often prefer using and maintaining their own saddles, bedrolls, bridles, and horsegear, though every rancher keeps a roomful of extra equipment. There are no set hours, no time clocks. Buckaroos live on the corporate or family ranch, and when the job needs to be done, it gets done. Some of the work ignores "work weeks," since hay harvest and roundup go nonstop. Factory workers in the city who dislike punching time clocks do not complain about the overtime wages those clocks dictate. There is no such thing as "working overtime" on a ranch. After long spans of long work days, though, a kind of compensatory time off can be taken on most ranches. The Fourth of July and Labor Day are traditional days off. Buckaroos are expected to take orders from and

Buckaroo Rusty McCorkle (center) with his family and a friend at breakfast time.

work side by side with the rancher and his family. Though they often buck authority, what they hate is not so much the issuance of labor commands as the way those instructions are sometimes given. It is not unlike the functioning of a small military unit, except here the troops can, and do, "up and quit" when things feel wrong. Buckaroos used to try to save up their earnings, hoping in some cases to make a payment on a small ranch of their own. But the economic conditions today, taken with the uncertainties of BLM management policies, means it is virtually impossible for a young man to make it—especially a family man. Not only would start-up require vast amounts of money and resources, but the available land is tied up. Most ranches are passed on within families or from family to family, or they are instantly bought up by established ranchers or a corporation or developer. So, like an able seaman who can never pilot his own ship, a buckaroo is unable to gain sufficient power and capital to run his own ranch. It may have always been that way in Nevada, because since the first phase of settlement the region has been almost entirely controlled by a few large corporations, several dozen families, and the United States Government.

The relationship between rancher and buckaroo is based on a traditional code of mutual trust, respect, and the essential honor in doing a good day's work for a good day's wages. Buckaroos are more likely to feel loyalty to the family ranch than to a large corporation owned by outsiders. Similarly, family ranchers are likely to be loyal to good hands. Honest, self-reliant buckaroos hold the entire industry together.

Many buckaroos lead the life because it is an alternative to what they know and want to leave behind. In this way, it is still the Real West, a mix of romantic belief and cold fact. This supposed escape from civilization that smacks of strength and freedom is an essential part of the appeal of the cowboy image and life—to them as well as to us. They are self-conscious players in the drama of the dusty, tough cattle business. The cowboy life stands for vigorous human liberty. At the same time, as one aging cowhand with back trouble said over and over again, the cowboy life is the dumps. A sense of exile links many working cowboys, as does a sense of quest and adventure. In various individual ways they have rejected or found uncomfortable other trades and professions. But though they are often noncomformists, most conform very strictly to their own community's expectations and customary legal system.

Some buckaroos are married, and some are not. Most working cowboys in earlier times were single, but today the number of married versus single men is about evenly split. The life is not conducive to raising families, and the buckaroo's rowdy ways and legendary flight from domesticity work against family life. There are some married buckaroos, however, who share a small house or mobile home with wife and children on their employer's ranch. In the future, there may be more such families on ranches, since there is a serious shortage of good hands, and ranch owners are increasingly willing to provide a home and benefits for a whole family in order to retain the services of proper laborers. Buckaroos with families tend to be more reliable employees and to stay longer. Single buckaroos live up to their famous penchant for moving on from time to time on impulse, after a quarrel with the boss, or in search of better wages.

Buckaroos tend not to be acquisitive or materialistic. Beyond a fine saddle (made by Ken Tipton in Winnemucca or at Capriola's in Elko) and good horse gear, some special possessions packed in a bedroll or war bag, and some household goods, no personal wealth will result from this work. Some of the men are mightily against the amassing of material things, which would be a hindrance to their self-reliant itinerant habits.

Is this a life of freedom? No—and yes. Buckaroos are trapped by wages, the environment, the nature of the labor, and the will of the current foreman. They are freed by the ability to choose where they work and what they do for a living. That kind of freedom attracts men to the work and serves as the core of the myth still sustaining the occupation. The years after the Civil War when the range cattle industry flourished saw the evolution of this cowboy trade and the simultaneous evolution of the glorified cowboy image. The symbols at the center of the myth do, after all, represent truth: buckaroos do have a kind of freedom, they do tend to be responsible though quixotic workers, they are surely rugged individualists, and their job provides them with a proximity to nature.

At the Ranch

Nature and weather control life in the range cattle industry as in farming; battles with foul weather and tough landscape are waged year in and year out. A rancher is almost completely dependent upon the natural water supply to keep the bunchgrass in the high country and in the desert growing and usable for his herds. "Bunchgrass" is both a particular small grass type and the general name for assorted hardy forage grasses like fescues and wheatgrass. He has more control on the home ranch, where the elaborate systems of flood irrigation channel water over fields of alfalfa and grains.

The pace of life on the ranch is slow. There are jobs like sitting on the back of a quarterhorse, meandering after cows nibbling grass under the sage. The alarm clock whines, you get up. When your work is done, you lie down. The daily cadence has been developed over years of experimentation and practice to find out what makes things work.

The cadence of the days then merges into the larger cadence of the seasons. The yearly round of life and work on Paradise Valley ranches runs like this: In the spring, there is calving, "turning out" of the herd onto federal grazing lands leased from the Bureau of Land Management (BLM), cultivation of crops, and irrigation of fields. Young cattle are branded and marked before being released on the grazing allotment with other cows. Experienced hands "start" colts on the path to becoming good cow ponies. In the summer, branding and marking continues, the cattle are moved from section to section of the BLM lands, then onto the higher U.S. Forest Service lands, and

96 Ranch buckaroos Clale Northrup, John DeHaan, Fred Stewart, and Chuck Wheelock at the Hartscrabble line camp.

96 Ranch crew from the 1979 fall trail drive at the Hartscrabble cabin: Paiute Indian buckaroos Tex Northrup, Myron Smart, and Theodore Brown; Mel Winslow, a friend; rancher Les Stewart and his son, Fred; neighboring rancher Henry Taylor and his son Clay.

the main hay crop is harvested and stored on the home ranch. Each Father's Day brings the main social event of the season, the annual Fireman's Bar-B-Cue hosted by the volunteer fire department in the valley. And the Fourth of July has always been a buckaroos' holiday. In the fall the cattle are "gathered" and driven from the high country back down to the home ranch. Buckaroos brand the missed cattle and select cows to be sold and shipped to market. Hunting and trapping seasons commence. The main autumn social occasion is the Fireman's Ball at the Odd Fellow's lodge hall. It is also county fair and rodeo season; in addition to large regional and national rodeos, there are occasional "ropings" held on family ranches like the 96. There are also "team roping" competitions, which differ from multievent rodeos. Here, two mounted riders work together in roping calves. There are team ropings at regular intervals from spring to fall, and the events are more for insiders than for outsiders. Winter is a time for catch-up chores about the home ranch, feeding cattle daily with the past summer's hay crop, and vacations and rest. There are more cattle to be sold and marketed. And there is the weather to be studied: will there be enough snow to replenish the valley's streams and water table? Throughout the year there are jobs that know no season too—the constant checking and doctoring of cattle and horses, periodic butchering of a steer for home range consumption, and routine maintenance of property and equipment.

The people of the region respect custom, order, and practical knowledge gained through apprenticeship and by following established techniques. It is a way of life that treasures and is given sustenance by old patterns of thought and attitude. But change has been continual, particularly in the technology of hay production and in the private use of public grazing lands. And in conveyences: the four-wheel-drive pickup truck is to some ranchers the most important development in their lifetimes.

There are several distinctions between ranching and farming. A small paradox: Ranchers are farmers, but farmers are not ranchers. Ranchers have always tilled the earth to a certain degree to produce grains and have worked hayfields in order to harvest the necessary feeds for cattle, horses, and mules. Among key factors separating "ranch" agriculture from "farm" agriculture are these:

1. Ranchers and their hired hands produce crops mainly for their own use on the home ranch. In a good year, a rancher may have an unusually abundant hay crop which allows him to market the surplus hay tonnage at distant points, but this is not usual. Ranchers customarily trade surplus hay bales to neighbors whose crops or supplies may be scant that season; this does not fall within the commercial sphere but is one of the ways ranchers cooperate for mutual aid and well-being.

2. Farms are commercial crop operations where the primary energies are funneled into growing and selling cash crops. Most farmers keep cattle, but the herds are usually considered secondary in importance to the farming operation, often indicating the farmer's desire for diversification. Farmers and ranchers harvest the same alfalfa, wheat, oats, and barley, but ranchers keep the crops for their own use, while farmers ship them to Winnemucca for sale and transportation to big city markets. Dairy cattle operations are farms, not ranches, since the essential product for market is milk, not livestock. Several old ranches in Humboldt County are now farming operations. This significant development is lamented by some ranchers, while it is heralded by others as a way of surviving in the future.

3. Ranches and farms have in their employ one or more wage-earning laborers. But their skills and characters tend to differ. Buckaroos farm, but farm hands do not buckaroo. The true buckaroo prefers working cattle on horseback. But during lengthy periods of the year buckaroos attend to agricultural equipment and the irrigation of hay fields for late summer harvest. Buckaroos maintain and operate modern haymaking machinery—combines, swathers, windrowers, balers, "harobeds," stack-retrievers, tractors—but most prefer cattle work. Buckaroos and farmhands, like ranchers and farmers, have had an uneasy relationship in the West. Along with sheepherders, farmers have in the past been in serious competition with ranchers for the land. Many Nevadans like to make distinctions between buckaroos and farm hands, though few express the difference as vividly as Pete Pedroli did during a visit in July 1978 at his ranch outside Winnemucca.

Dick Ahlborn: Well, I'd like to ask you one other question. Could you tell the difference between a buckaroo and a farmer, just by walking down the street?

Pedroli: Yeah, you could always tell the difference.

Ahlborn: How?

Pedroli: The way he walked. Buckaroo was generally stoved up from sittin' on a horse so damn long. The farmer, he was generally stoved up from goin' over the clods and the dirt followin' the plow.

Tex Northrup

Buckaroos Chuck Wheelock and John DeHaan at the front gate of the 96 Ranch.

The image outsiders have of cattle ranches populated by tough cowboys on wild ponies wrestling mean longhorn bulls is not altogether correct. Television shows like "Bonanza," "Gunsmoke," and "Big Valley," and the countless Western movies seldom give us a glimpse of buckaroos sweating over a blown-out diesel tractor tire or heaving wet hay bales. Unfortunately for our conceptions of buckarooing in the West, we know little about these men in that large part of their lives spent fussing with balky combine engines or mending endless miles of barbed wire fence, doctoring edgy cows with injection guns filled with vitamins and serums, or working through stacks of government regulations and tax forms. The reality of western ranching life and the buckaroo business was lost in the mythology and legend that began a hundred years ago.

Some observers think that farming is the wave of the future in the arid West, thanks to new strategies of land preparation and irrigation; indeed it is likely to become increasingly difficult for the family ranch to maintain itself by raising cattle alone. Ranchers customarily paint a dark picture of the future of their business. Carlo Recanzone and his son Butch, who as a young man hopes to continue operation of their pioneer family ranch, agree that their future is in the government's hands. They can make it, they say, but there will be significant changes. In an optimistic mood Butch says, "Ranchers are known to be survivors." One of the strengths of western ranching families is that they are inheritors and conscious curators of a significant piece of the real and mythic American past. They know that the past of gritty pioneers and greedy exploiters lives visibly and immediately in their present. A family ranch is a living family album, and in its story are lines from every history book about what America is.

B Irons

Branding livestock is an essential piece of work performed by ranchers and buckaroos. A brand is the special mark or identifying design owned by a rancher and used in registering and identifying his cattle and horses. A branding iron is the handmade iron or steel tool that applies the mark to the beast. The end with the owner's brand is pressed against the side of the animal after being heated to red hot in a fire in the corral. The earliest "irons," as they are called in Nevada, were simple initials, figures, or numbers, but the designs grew intricate and ingenious as generations passed and conflicts arose over duplications of simple figures. The iron designs are recorded in a statewide brand book published by the Nevada Department of Agriculture, which often provides the ultimate evidence of ownership in disputes. The brands are illustrated, previous owners are listed, and the location of the mark on the animal is given. Brand books also indicate other ownership marks—wattles and ear notches. "Irons" are serious business.

Each community has its own state-operated and employed brand inspector, often a rancher who inspects cattle on a part-time basis. The inspector is charged with overseeing the shipment of certified cattle by ensuring proper ownership; he sometimes arbitrates in brand identification problems. Identification of brands on cattle is usually simple, but it can be difficult if the irons were applied carelessly or improperly. When the same brand is held by different ranchers, for various reasons, it must be applied on specific sides or parts of the cattle to keep things straight.

Cattle branding is done mainly at two times of the year, in the spring after calving and in the fall after the roundup and driving the herd back to the home ranch for winter. The fall branding serves to locate and mark any calves born in the summer range or yearlings missed in the spring work. The work is traditionally done "outside" by roping the cows from horseback, throwing them, and slapping the hot iron on. It is a chore relished by many buckaroos. Some ranchers now use "squeeze chutes" (metal contraptions that are placed at a corner of a corral or pen to trap and hold the cow firmly while the iron is applied) and the latest electric branders. Other important tasks are performed at the same time as branding: castration, ear marking, wattling, dehorning, and the administration of vaccinations, medicine, or vitamin serums with modern injection guns. All six pieces of work can be done in quick succession by several men working as a team. One person ropes and throws the cow and holds the rope taut. A second person lops a piece of ear off with a pocket knife while holding the cow's head down with one knee. That "knife man" (man or women) can then move around to accomplish castration (if necessary) and also cut the wattle mark. In ear marking, a crop, slit, split, or bob of the cow's ear is made with the penknife blade, and portions of the ear are removed or cut according to the established precedent in the brand book. The wattle is a special knife cut on the fatty portion of the cow's neck, jaw, or brisket area; the cut hide heals and hangs down in a certain position. Like the iron itself, ear mark styles and wattles are considered a rancher's property and can be used by other ranchers only if purchased and duly recorded with the state brand inspector's office. Ear marks and wattles are efficient identification methods in foul weather, under dusty conditions, or when cows are bunched up together. The law requires marking cattle with branding irons, and the customary legal system based on traditional usage since the middle of the nineteenth century calls for ear notching and wattling. Some ranchers use modern plastic tags secured to the cow's ear instead of the knife cut; the tags come in different colors and carry numbers and identification codes. All ranchers brand cattle, and most ranchers brand their horses too. Some ranchers also ear mark and wattle their cattle.

There are conventions in brand choice and design based on practicality and economy. A design should not blotch, so the iron or steel that will touch the cow's hide has to be a certain thickness, about one-eighth to one-quarter inch. Thinner irons would slice through the hide and injure the animal, and wider irons would dull the design. A plain design further reduces the blotching problem. The best iron designs are simply but ingeniously created to represent the owner's ranch or name. Good brands are also simple enough

Two teams work to brand, castrate, ear mark, wattle, dehorn, and vaccinate calves near a Circle A line camp.

to discourage thieves and rustlers from being tempted to change the mark with "running irons." Running irons are kept by ranchers and used to mark strays when necessary, or to put a neighbor's brand on his strays that drift into the wrong herd. In addition, some now use "year irons," which apply a single digit brand indicating the year; for example, "4" indicates 1974, "9" indicates 1979.

Irons are read from top to bottom, left to right, and from outside in. Many irons are easy to read, like the Stewarts' 96 iron, a pioneer brand Mr. Stewart's grandfather bought from Aaron Denio when they took over the Denio ranch adjoining on the south. "The 96" is a major family ranch in Paradise, and the iron is well known throughout the Great Basin. Increasing in complexity are irons that have a "bar," "slash," "bench," "rocker," "circle," "three-quarter circle," "quarter circle," "wings," "box," "diamond," "rafter," and other conventional symbols that are attached in various ways to the core of the brand—an initial, a number, a figure.

In a hypothetical case of iron design, the first

pioneer who stakes out the land and starts building the ranch might simply use his last initial—say, *M*. He finds that something more is necessary, since a new ranch over the mountain has the same iron, and furthermore, a ranch in the next county has the W iron. Careless or inexperienced hands have been known inadvertently to apply his M iron upside down in the flurry and confusion of the branding activities. So he adds a rafter over the initial, creating the Rafter M iron: Later, one of his sons decides to go into the cattle business and wants to register his own brand but stay on the home ranch with the family elders and eventually take over the operation when the old man retires. So, the young man registers his own iron, which he calls the Diamond M: made by welding another piece of iron onto the rafter. One or two additions are usually the limit before completely new irons are concocted. Ranchers may own several irons at once, since neighbors and other herds are occasionally bought out and added.

In Paradise Valley, these are some of the irons on some of the ranches we became acquainted with:

Now owned by the Nevada First Corporation, this iron is called the "Circle A" locally and was registered by an early cattle corporation, Abel and Curtner. It is thought that it was originally called Compass, but there was some conflict with local Masons over its use, so it began to be called "Circle A." It is one of those irons with a common name that does not quite match the symbol itself.

The 7 U P iron is well-known as the Boggio brand, and Joe Boggio's son Harold now owns it. Even when an iron passes down within the same family, the symbol is re-registered with the state.

Seven H L Combined, an original 1864 iron of the Lye brothers, is now owned by Keith and Jean Thomas who operate the venerable pioneer Lye ranch at the head of Indian Creek.

C Bar, the iron owned by Bob Cassinelli and his sons, Bob, Pete, Dan, and Don.

Loui Cerri's Inverted T N T Combined.

Stan and Janice M. Klaumann's Four R Combined.

Quartercircle Hanging H, owned by Elizabeth Miller.

101 The 101, a pioneer brand invented by the patriarch of a German family, Gerhard Miller, Sr. The 101 is a popular iron in the West, but there is no connection between this one and the 101 Ranch in Oklahoma, founded in the 1890s by Col. George Miller. The Paradise Valley 101 was recently sold by Alvin E. and Anesita E. Miller to a young rancher from Turlock, California, Steve Lucas.

Carlo A. Recanzone of the pioneer Home Ranch, begun in 1864, has the Open A 9, which he registered in 1939 when he took principal leadership of the family operation.

Carlo's son, Carlo J. (Butch) Recanzone registered his iron with a symbol that cleverly coincides with his father's brand, to make the bond closer and make identification of Recanzone stock simple. He calls it the 6 V.

Keystone, owned by Lyman W. Schwartz, grandson of pioneer businessman and rancher Robert Schwartz, a German immigrant.

The 96 iron used by the Stewart family on 96 Ranch cattle.

Several of the irons can be read correctly upside down, making the concentrated work of cattle branding a bit less troublesome: the 101, the 96, the Inverted T N T Combined, the Seven H L Combined, Fred and Robert Buckingham's Reverse B B Combined ( ), and Jose Gastañaga's Seven X L( ).

A surprisingly ancient custom (performed by Egyptians four thousand years ago and spread throughout the globe), branding cattle and horses is of extreme importance in the range cattle industry. It is not required on ranches and farms where the herd is kept inside fenced lots and controlled pastures, but the use of the iron is mandatory in the West where cattle graze out on the range. It is a rigidly enforced custom that answers both official legal orders and the unofficial, traditional legal system within the community. The official code combined with the unwritten laws of custom help keep life peaceful and orderly. It is hard to imagine the buckaroo life and work without the branding scene.

OVERLEAF:
Branding at the 96 Ranch.

Clothing

Like the many costumes worn by Americans for the performance of different jobs and chosen roles in society, the cowboy's clothing is distinctive. It developed according to the requirements of the profession —boots, chaps, neckerchiefs—but with a certain style of its own that is particularly "American" and more particularly "western." The western style of cut and cloth is periodically fashionable in other parts of the country, and another wave of western fashion is upon us, with "designer jeans" and Tony Lama boots propped on Wall Street walnut desks. While certain features of cowboy clothes come from necessary function, like the heels on boots, other features are more aesthetic and symbolic than practical, like pearl snaps on shirts. For young men in the West, becoming a buckaroo is greatly enhanced by the image of manliness, vigor, and pride the special clothing conveys.

They could just as easily wear suit coats, vests, plain shirts, small felt hats, and "work shoes" like the buckaroos in the 1890s. Fashions change for traditional working people as well as for the city's upper crust. The Angora "wooly" chaps once standard in Nevada gave way to "batwings," which gave way about thirty years ago to today's short, fringed "chinks." Jeans are still worn, but a good pair of brown Sears work pants or Big Smith overalls would probably serve as well. Ranchers and cowboys who are secure and reasonably content with their way of life prefer to dress according to the standards and traditions of the community. A feeling of belonging and mutual respect is more important to people in Nevada than a feeling of being different. Clothes are yet another way of expressing one's role in society and one's acceptance or rejection of a community's traditions and habits. In Paradise Valley first impressions are important, and character judgments are often formed quickly on the perception of a stranger's appearance.

Clothes that are too fancy or expensive-looking are avoided by most experienced buckaroos, even when getting cleaned up and going into Winnemucca for an evening or special occasion. You can tell a newcomer or outsider by the clothes he wears, and the old hands reveal subtly the correct standards and customs to a new man in the outfit. Certain variations may be significant only to insiders. For example, a cowboy's place of origin and mode of upbringing and training in the profession can often be determined by the style of the heel of the boot, or by the manner of wearing jeans—very long or shorter, tucked inside the boot tops or left out. A cowboy from the Nevada tradition believes that wearing jeans very long outside the boot keeps dust and pests out. Another man, from Montana, perhaps, believes pant legs have to be tucked inside the boot tops for the same reasons.

Hats, too, help determine origin. Shapes and styles of cowboy hats change according to a regional sense of fashion, and young men are always particular about hat shape and style. Older men care less about it, and since years ago hat brims were narrower and crowns lower, any hat like that (worn by a man aged fifty up) is called an "old man hat." Buckaroos hate being caught without their hats planted on their heads. Hats are permanent fixtures, essential equipment not to be fiddled with too much. Some oldtime cowhands believe that decorating hats with ornaments of any kind bespoils them, but others, like Chuck Wheelock, feel funny wearing a hat without a tail feather from a cock pheasant sticking out behind the hatband. A buckaroo usually has at least two hats, both expensive. One is worn every day, all day, indoors and out. The second hat is kept in a box at home and fetched out for special occasions like a cattleman's association meeting, a birthday party, a big dance, a BLM meeting at the Humboldt County Library, or the Fireman's Bar-B-Cue each June. Every man's hat is given a particular pinch, roll, or wrinkle to make it his own. The same hat is generally worn until it wears out, and a man riding horseback with cattle can be easily identified through the dust and haze by the outline of his head and hat. A good, expensive hat is highly prized today just as it has always been, and some ranchers' organizations present fine new hats as special awards, the way big rodoes give the all-around champion a fine new saddle.

In the past few years, caps or "cat hats" have grown in popularity in Nevada as elsewhere, and some men wear cat hats instead of cowboy hats. Cat hats are synthetic fabric, shaped like baseball caps with a bill on the front, and emblazoned with some sort of emblem such as Caterpillar (hence "cat hat"), John Deere, Powder River, or Eagle Claw Hooks. Cat hats are worn almost exclusively during periods of work on the ranch, but usually not when riding and tending cattle. For example, young Fred Stewart of the 96 Ranch wears a cat hat when working on farm machines or running equipment on the home ranch,

Herb Pembroke, Dave Hiller, and Dick Gusky at the Little Owyhee line camp.

but always wears his black felt cowboy hat when working cattle on horseback.

Neckerchiefs are another distinctive part of the buckaroo's outfit. The blue or red-and-white patterned neckerchiefs sported by dudes at eastern square dances are not found in Nevada on working cowboys. They seem more suitable for farmers or railroad men, or as pocket handkerchiefs. Moreover, the kind that can be bought at the local dimestore is really too small to be worn in the Nevada tradition, where they are wrapped around the neck twice and then tied in a small knot in the front. Buckaroos and their wives sometimes make these functional and distinctive neckerchiefs by purchasing a large piece of soft cloth (about three square yards) in town and then cutting and edging it to the individual's preferred size, but most men buy them in the women's scarves section in stores like The Stockmen's in Winnemucca. Called "neckerchief," "scarf," "wild rag," "glad rag," or "bandanna," this basic item can be plain black or a brilliantly colored print.

Chaps, from the Mexican-Spanish *chaparreras,* are leather leg coverings of various styles worn by working buckaroos when riding in brush or sage, for warmth in the winter, and for "show" in rodeos or parades. There are several different styles: "shotguns," "woolies" ("hair chaps"), "batwings," and "chinks," reflecting different regional traditions as well as changing fashions and personal preferences within the same region. The oldstyle shotgun chaps were never very popular in Paradise Valley. They are straight, plain, narrow, and completely enwrap the rider's legs from belt to boot sole. They have to be stepped into and pulled up over the jeans. The buckaroos we visited who wore shotguns generally had a pair of chinks as well. Another old form, the semi-shotgun style woolies of Angora goat skin with the fleece out, were widely used in northern Nevada from early times into recent years. In their time, Angora woolies were popular for their warmth and comfort, their appearance and ability to "turn the storm." They were in turn replaced by leather batwing chaps which fitted loosely but fully covered the legs, waist to ankle, and were wrapped around the rider's jean legs and strapped or buckled behind. Batwings are rare in this region, but Harold Chapin, a well-known rodeo champion and former herd boss for the McCleary Cattle Company in Paradise Valley, likes to wear a special pair of thin, floppy, fancy "bronc chaps" that are cut like batwings when he competes in a rodeo. The newest style, which has been popular for more than fifty years, is called chinks. Chinks are short, fringed chaps that reach below the knee and are often open behind the leg. Rancher Les Stewart explained their development in a letter in January 1979. I had asked him if chinks could have come from a Mexican tradition, since one of the buckaroos we visited told us they were from the Spanish "chinquederos." Beyond our not discovering any such word in Spanish, old or new, Mr. Stewart said that

> *Chinks probably originated when a buckaroo's old chaps became well worn and frayed and in an attempt to salvage something and save the cost of new ones, he trimmed them down until "chinks" were all that remained. Then the idea caught on and the style became popular. I think their origin is as unromantic as that, purely a practical evolution. They are just chinks, "chinquederos" is getting far too sophisticated.*

The word "chinks" may have come from Spanish words *chingo* (leather stirrup covers) or *chingadera* ("cut off, blunted"), but the derivation is still unproven. Today, some people still make their own chinks from a wornout pair of shotguns or batwings. But more people make chinks and other chaps from scratch, like Chuck Wheelock, Henry Taylor, and Butch Recanzone, who made his first pair of chinks by taking the pattern off his father's. Butch made a fancy pair carrying the ranch's 6 V iron for his father as a Christmas present in 1978. He says that they are not difficult to make; all you need is some leather, two needles, a sharp awl, and heavy waxed thread. It is "Something to do on a winter's night."

In Paradise Valley, as in other small communities, everyone dresses much the same. Wild outfits indicate a strong ego or eccentricity of some sort. These "dude outfits" will not do for the average citizen, though they are permissible on special occasions. As Pete Pedroli told Dick Ahlborn, a buckaroo's clothing should not be "too fancy for us sagebrush boys." Everyday dress gives little sign of social standing, financial power, or status. The key to picking out clothes is conservative practicality matched against the prevailing standards of the region.

Bunkhouses and Line Camp Cabins

Bunkhouses shelter buckaroos. The same shelter may be called by different names, depending on location and use: bunkhouse, cabin, line camp, buckaroo camp, cow camp. A bunkhouse is usually thought of as a small house on the home ranch that serves as a permanent home for employees, whether buckaroos or hands. With one or more rooms, there is space for cooking, eating, sleeping, and storing horsegear and equipment. Ranch hands and buckaroos call this dwelling home for the duration of their employment. Temporary shelters are also placed strategically at great distances from the home ranch and in the privately owned fields enclosed in BLM or Forest Service grazing lands. These are the line camps, buckaroo camps, or cow camps where men stay for short periods of time while tending cattle through the government grazing allotments "on the mountain." *Line camp* refers to both the building and the place. Some line camps are canvas wall tents right on the ground, some are wall tents with raised wood platform floors and frames, and some are beautifully constructed granite buildings made with more care than many modern homes in Winnemucca.

Few bunkhouses or line camps were built and used by the early pioneers, since in the beginning few extra employees were kept by the family ranchers. Most ranchers had large families, and with the help

The Circle A Quinn River line camp cabin.

of neighbors during seasons of peak activity—calving, branding, haying round-up, shipping—they could marshal sufficient hands to get the work done. As ranchers gradually built up the range cattle industry and their herds grew in size, itinerant buckaroos began staying beyond particular seasons and required special housing both on the home ranch and in the desert and mountain grazing areas. Paradise Valley was settled in the 1860s, and the first special-purpose bunkhouses were like the one built on Aaron Denio's homestead of adobe bricks in about 1870, on property now used as a "hay camp" on the Stewart ranch. The early Italian masons built no stone bunkhouses or camps at first. Their energies went into the main house, horse barns, and granaries and into developing their agricultural and cattle-raising enterprises. They found time to build stone bunkhouses when their first responsibilities were met and when changing work patterns in later years made the construction of bunkhouses necessary.

Specialists who study traditional architecture spend more time and effort documenting the buildings' details and history and less on trying to place them in styles or periods of architecture. Unlike academic

Herb Pembroke at the Little Owyhee line camp cabin.

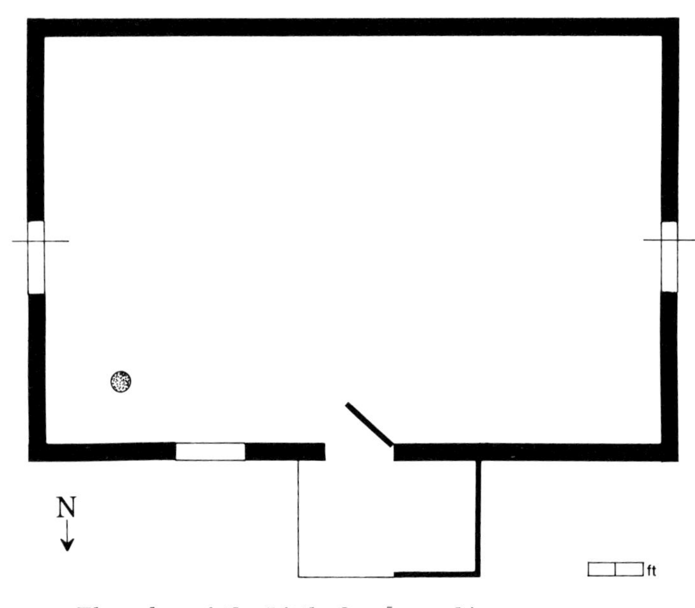

Floorplan of the Little Owyhee cabin.

architecture, folk buildings are the result of generations of experiment, use, and custom and pay less attention to popular trends and fashions. Like ballads, or legends of Butch Cassidy's escape from Winnemucca, or ways to make biscuits over a sagebrush fire, folk buildings are expressions of the region and the people's heritage, as settlers carve out shelters in the new landscape. Architecture specialists study four aspects of a building (in addition to history): form, construction, use, and decoration. Dimensions and floorplan (form) place folk buildings in a classification of similar types, which can show regional distribution and traditionality. Construction methods indicate not only the builder's origins and craftsmanship but his way of coping with the new land and its possibilities for creating architecture. Understanding the function of a building helps us know more about the people who built it, and details of ornament or decoration indicate the effect that some period of national taste or style has had in the region or community.

The dwellings and temporary shelters of working cowboys fall into different categories of traditional structures. There are three types of bunkhouses and buckaroo camps in northern Nevada—two house types well known in other parts of North America, and one type introduced into this region by Alpine Italian masons.

The first of the three types of dwellings represents the modern continuation of a house form known for hundreds of years in Europe, the single-pen house. Built either square or slightly rectangular, it developed in its present size and shape in the Middle Ages and was brought from the British Isles to the American colonies in the East by the first settlers. It is found all over the United States, constructed of various materials: heavy timber in New England, red brick in the Chesapeake-Tidewater, stone in Pennsylvania, round logs in the Deep South, hewn logs in the Midwest, light frame everywhere. In Nevada this venerable house type is found built in sod and adobe by the first pioneers and in stone and frame by later ranchers. The single-pen house type is exemplified by the cabin at the Little Owyhee line camp ("the Circle A"), the bunkhouse at the Bradshaw-Cerri-Wallace place, and the house from the Mill Ranch that has been reconstructed as part of the "Buckaroo" exhibit at the National Museum of History and Technology.

This house form is the basic building block for most American folk house types. Its prime features are its one-room square or rectangular shape with the door in a long side and a gable roof. Though scholars call this house a "single-pen" house, the people who make and use them just call them cabins or houses.

The second type of bunkhouse is actually a version of the single-pen house, but the house plan has been turned and the door placed in the gable end rather than in one of the long sides. The placement of the door in the gable may reflect Greek Revival and carpenter Gothic styles of the late nineteenth century in the West. There are numerous examples of this end-opening single-pen house type; good ones include the Stewart ranch bunkhouse, the Ferraro-Zatica/Gavica-Cassinelli bunkhouse, and the cabin on the Boggio property. Bunkhouses of this form are usually frame, but the Boggio cabin (on property leased to the Klaumanns) was built by Italian stonemasons of sawn sandstone. Both of the single-pen forms (side-opening and end-opening) are often divided into two small rooms inside, but the general rule calls for one open room. Sometimes the second type is added onto for

Sandstone buckaroo camp on Boggio property rented by the Klaumann family.

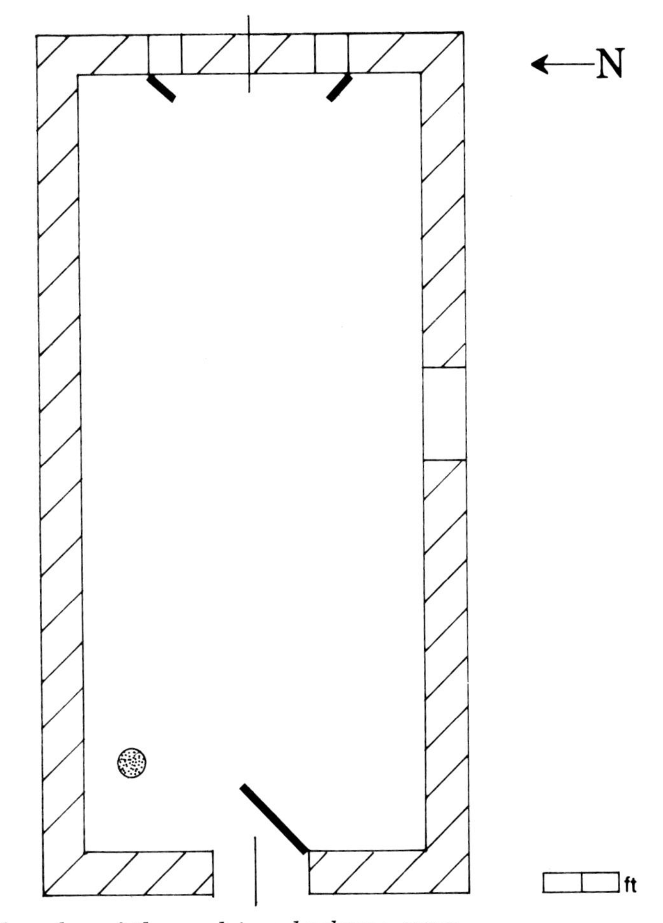

Floorplan of the sandstone buckaroo camp.

Granite bunkhouse on the Recanzone Home Ranch.

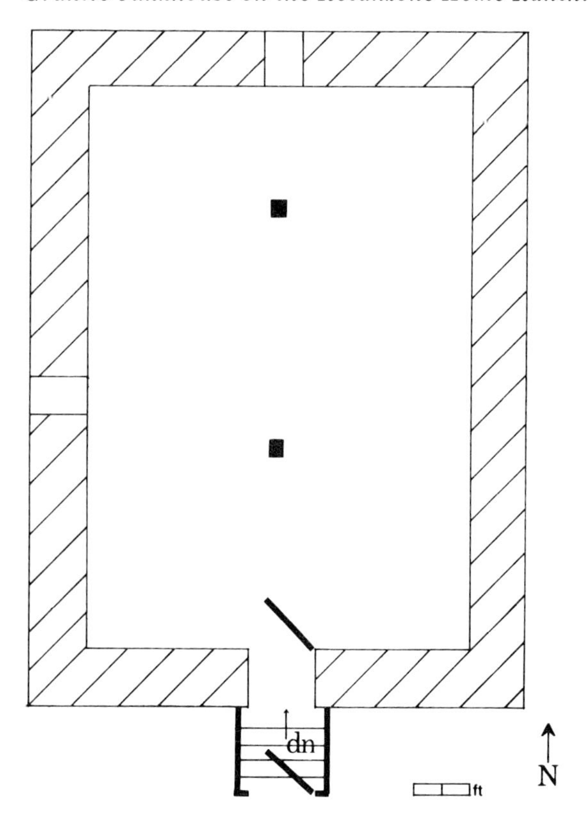

Floorplan of the Recanzone granite bunkhouse, cellar.

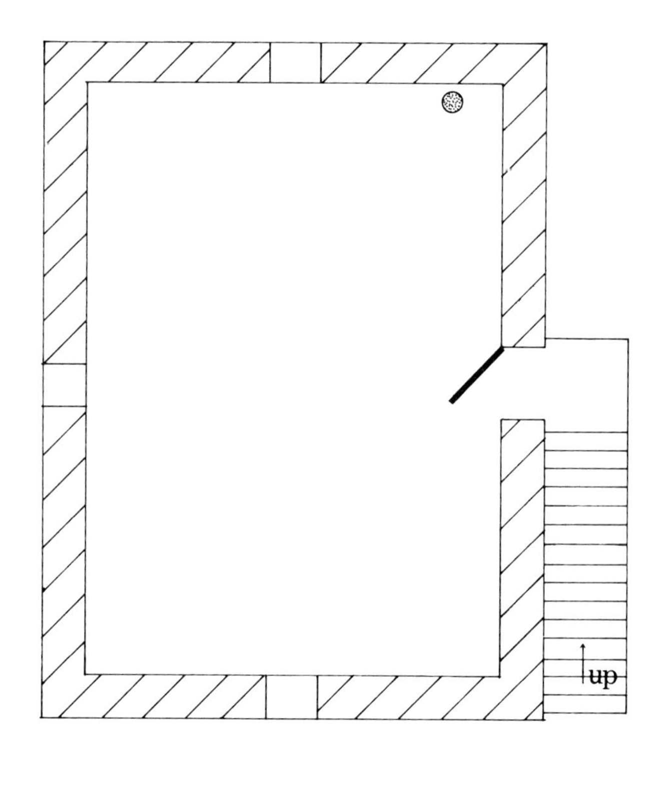

Floorplan of the Recanzone granite bunkhouse, living quarters, upper level.

more sleeping rooms, as with the Stewart and Schwartz bunkhouses.

Line-camp cabins may be either of those two main forms. On the 96 Ranch property there are several line-camp cabins in both frame and stone. The Bradshaw field cabin and the Hartscrabble cabin are made of granite, and both were built by Italian stonemason Antone Ramasco about 1920. They are single-pen houses of the first type, but with shed roofs rather than gable roofs. At Cold Springs camp and Black Ridge camp, Les Stewart built frame cabins for the buckaroos; Cold Springs is of the second type (end-opening) and Black Ridge is of the first (door in the long side).

The third type of bunkhouse consists of two-level buildings of stone designed and built by immigrant masons from the foot of the Italian Alps. Several outstanding examples are in use today in Paradise. The first floor is partly underground and houses a cellar or meat room, and the buckaroos and ranch hands live in the second story, reached by an outdoor staircase. They are roughly square with thick rock walls, generally have a hip roof, and were built by several specialists in the Ferrarro, Recanzone, and Ramasco families. The best of the Ramasco masons, Antone Ramasco, was the acknowledged master of stonemasonry in the valley, though other Italians like Steve Boggio and Virgil Pasquale did important work, too. Rather than convert to a rancher or businessman like other Italians, Antone Ramasco remained a builder all his life, and his expertise and personal mortaring style are evident on many buildings in Humboldt County today. The sandstone bunkhouse at the Bull Head Ranch is a masterpiece, as are the two huge granite horse barns at the 96 Ranch, built by Ramasco with his brother-in-law Charlie Zorio. The Italian masons got their soft sandstone (easily cut with a hand saw or special hatchet) from a quarry site on the east edge of the valley on the desert's apron, while the granite came (with considerably more effort) from a quarry up Lamance Creek at the western edge where the Santa Rosa Range rises.

The bunkhouse in the exhibition was acquired from Bob Cassinelli, whose family has operated the Mill Ranch for some years. It was built for John Schneider in about 1921. Schneider was an immigrant German trapper who came to the ranch in the 1920s and stayed on as a ranch hand and jack-of-all-trades. Called "Coyote John" or "Hans," Schneider was well-known in the county in his later years working for Lorenzo Recanzone at the Mill Ranch.

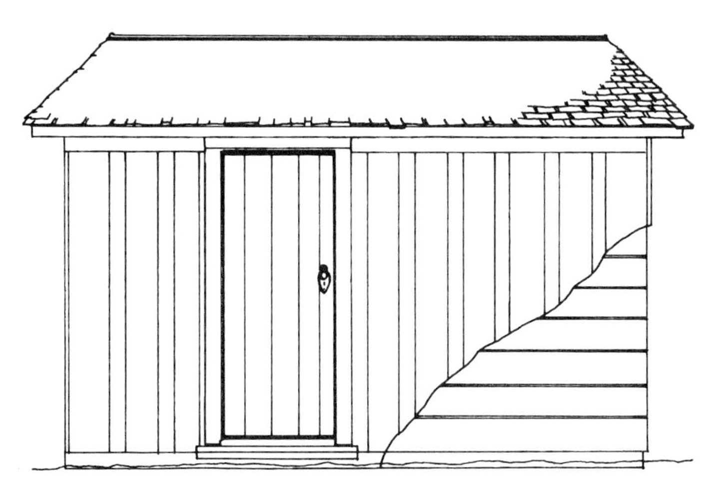

Schneider house, wall construction revealed.

John Schneider's home on its site at the Mill Ranch.

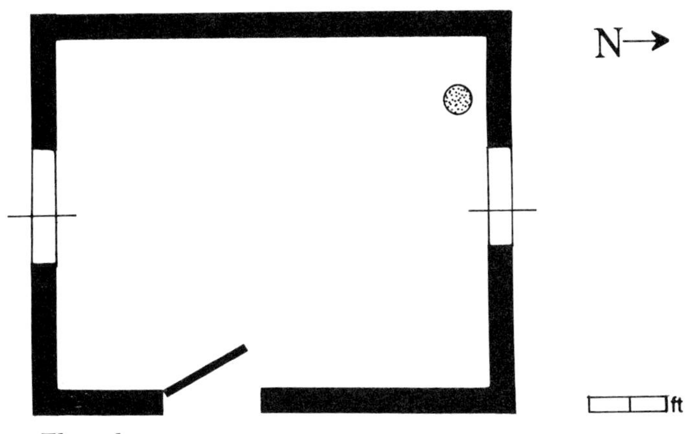

Floorplan

The Mill Ranch. John Schneider's bunkhouse is the small, dark building in the center of the photograph.

Schneider became an informal member of the Recanzone family, who found in him a stout worker and loyal friend who was able to protect the Recanzone women and children when the men were working away from the ranch. Carlo Recanzone remembers from his childhood at the Mill Ranch when Schneider chased a threatening stranger away with his trusty "thirty-thirty" Winchester. And when Lorenzo Recanzone took the whole family back to Italy and France in 1919 to deliver a deceased relative to the old country, Schneider was put in charge of the ranch. A substantial amount of money was put in the bank in Winnemucca in Schneider's name, to be used as needed. When the family returned to Paradise not one dollar had been spent. Trustworthy men like Schneider had a strong role in rearing the youngsters and passing on knowledge of the ranch life and work. Carlo and his sister Angie Recanzone Genasci fondly recall "old Hans." As Carlo put it, "Old John was a grand ole guy for us." Schneider died in 1932 at the age of ninety and is buried in the Paradise community cemetery near the Recanzone family plots.

The dwelling typifies the form of bunkhouses and line camps across the West. It was built in a distinctive mode common for small frame buildings in some sections of the nineteenth-century West. Called "single-wall construction" by people in Nevada, this framing technique uses no vertical bracing but depends instead on a strong wall of large vertical boards made rigid by the roof system. Second and third layers of battens, horizontal boards, and interior insulation are usually added. Recanzone hired a carpenter named Teddy Weller to build the house for Schneider, who had been living in a wall tent with a board floor —a chilly dwelling in wintertime. It was built on wooden skids or runners so that the building could be dragged to different parts of the ranch according to Schneider's duties of the season or year.

In the building's later history at the Mill Ranch, it served as a bunkhouse and as a store room for fence materials, tools, branding irons, and other supplies kept under lock and key.

Most buckaroos today live in modern mobile homes or prefabricated houses on the home ranches, provided by the ranchers mainly because there are so many married men needing separate dwellings. Most of the old bunkhouses where several single buckaroos lived together are now vacant and used as saddle rooms or storage sheds. But on the larger outfits like Nevada Vaca, Nevada Garvey, and the 96 Ranch, the traditional bunkhouses are maintained and in use both on the home ranch and out on the summer range —at line camps many miles from the ranch headquarters.

"Coyote" John Schneider and one of the Recanzone family, probably during the 1920s.

John Schneider's bunkhouse is at the heart of the buckaroo exhibition. It is a tangible artifact that exemplifies an important mode of wooden carpentry in the West. It is a traditional dwelling rooted in the cultural landscape on a family ranch and represents the way many cowmen and ranch hands live, yesterday and today. Numbered in the catalog, it is an exhibit artifact of larger dimension and of major significance both as an individual sample of folk housing and as a reconstructed context for a constellation of other artifacts from northern Nevada.

Exhibition Catalogue

RICHARD E. AHLBORN

The exhibition entitled "Buckaroos in Paradise" consists of more than two hundred artifacts from northern Nevada. Each object has direct associations with Paradise Valley, the focus of the American Folklife Center's Paradise Valley Folklife Project.

Most of the artifacts were borrowed, purchased, or donated from people living in northern Nevada. They were chosen to represent the variety of objects that touch the daily life of the buckaroo, or to represent part of his historical background. The objects, however, do not appear in quantities proportional to their present-day use, nor can two hundred artifacts represent the entire range of subtypes of object classes. Thus, the two center-fired saddles symbolize many other single- as well as double-rigged saddles familiar to the buckaroo of northern Nevada.

The artifact entries are grouped into three main topics and numbered sequentially from 1 through 244: "Background to the Buckaroo Life," "Tools and Crafts," and "Bunkhouse." Each of these topics is divided in the catalogue into four or more subtopics such as "foodways," "blacksmithing," or "costume." In each catalogue entry, the description and date of the artifact is followed by its size in inches and centimeters and by the initials of the lender or of the appropriate division of the National Museum of History and Technology:

J/G B	Joe and Geraldine Boggio, Winnemucca, Nevada
RC	Robert Cassinelli, Paradise Valley, Nevada
M/W F	Marguerite (Mrs. Leonard) Faupel and son, Wesley Faupel, Winnemucca
W/I F	Walter and Irene Fischer, Paradise Valley
HM	Howard W. Marshall, Alexandria, Virginia
AM	Alvin Miller, Paradise Valley
FM	Fred L. Miller, Paradise Valley
PP	Melvin "Pete" Pedroli, Winnemucca
L/M S	Leslie and Marie Stewart, Paradise Valley
DZ	Delfina (Mrs. John) Zatica, Paradise Valley
NMHT	National Museum of History and Technology
CG	Division of Ceramics and Glass
CL	Division of Community Life
C	Division of Costume
DL	Division of Domestic Life
EI	Division of Extractive Industries

Many other people in Nevada provided information on the buckaroo's artifacts and life, for which I am deeply grateful. The Smithsonian exhibition was designed by Deborah M. Bretzfelder, and my efforts were greatly assisted by Dr. Elizabeth M. Harris, Thomas N. Tully, Charles H. Rowell, Dr. Thomas E. Chávez, Suzanna Spencer, and Hazel Covert.

Tex Northrup

Background to the Buckaroo Life

Local and Family History

1. ADOBE BRICK

Molded, sun-dried mud bricks were made in Paradise Valley; these were used in the Lye butcher shop about 1875.

H 2½ in/6.4 cm; L 8¼ in/21 cm; D 4¼ in/10.9 cm (NMHT-CG 1980.0019.1). HM

2. LITHOGRAPH OF EARLY RANCH

"Grain and Stock Ranch of Carrel and Stock Paradise Valley." Printed about 1880 by Britton and Rey of San Francisco, this view is typical of commercially published county histories.

H 12¾ in/32.4 cm; W 15¼ in/38.8 cm. L/M S

3

3, 4. PORTRAITS OF EARLY SETTLERS

Fredrick William Stock and wife, Wilhelmina Wahague, taken about 1890. Photographs mounted in molded plaster frames graced the homes of successful pioneer families throughout the West. Born in 1837 in Hesse-Kassel, Stock anglicized his given names before arriving in Nevada from California.

H 34 in/86.3 cm; W 30 in/76.2 cm. L/M S

5. CHEST

Used to store clothes, coverlets, books, and toys for more than eighty years, the trunk was made by local buckaroo "Dutch John" Goeppner. He used imported factory-made hinges, nails, and locks; the pine boards, wrought iron handles, tin reinforcers, and cowhide seals were obtained locally.

L 31½ in/79.4 cm; H and D 18 in/45.7 cm. L/M S

5

6

6. SIDE CHAIR WITH THONG SEAT

Based on a European folk design, the slat or ladder-back side chair was often given a laced rawhide thong seat in America. This repainted example was probably made between 1880 and 1910.

H 33½ in/85.1 cm; seat to floor H 15 in/38.1 cm; Seat: W 18½ in/47 cm; D 14½/36.8 cm. L/M S

7. WALL CABINET ON BRACKETS

Probably made in the area about 1890, the cabinet reflects Germanic design and indicates the common ailments of frontier life through its medicinal contents (items 8-17).

H 68 in/172.8 cm; W 36½ in/92.7 cm; D 13½ in/34.3 cm. L/M S

CONTAINERS FOR MEDICINES IN CABINET

8. "VICKS VAPORUB" JAR

Used as decongestant. About 1950.

H 2½ in/6.3 cm; Diam 1⅝ in/4.1 cm. L/M S (8–13)

9. POWDERED ALUM BOX

Used as gargle and douche. About 1960.

H 2⅞ in/7.4 cm; Diam 1⅞ in/4.8 cm.

7

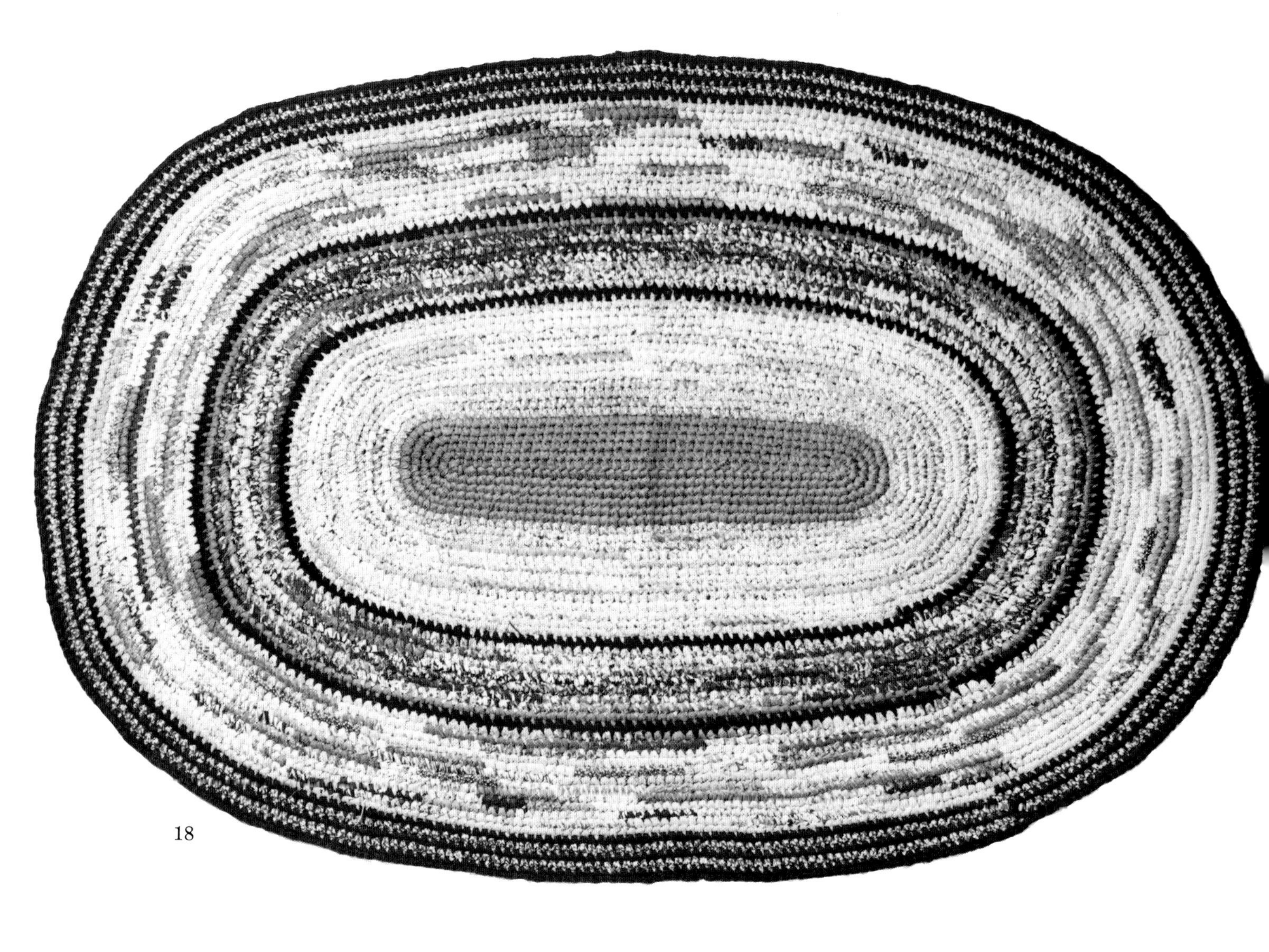

18

10. "OURINE" BOX AND BOTTLE

Used for sore ears. About 1960.

Box: H 4⅛ in/10.5 cm; W 2⅞ in/7.4 cm; D 1¾ in/4.5 cm.

11. "MITCHELL" ESSENCE GINGER BOX

Used as a decongestant. About 1950.

Box: H 6⅜ in/16.2 cm; W 2¼ in/5.8 cm; D 1¼ in/3.2 cm.

12. "VASELINE" JELLY (IN TIN BOX)

Used as lubricant. About 1940.

H 3¼ in/8.3 cm; W and D 3⅝ in/9.2 cm.

13. ATOMIZER

Glass and "Vulcanite." About 1950.

L 5⅝ in/14.3 cm; H 2⅜ in/6 cm; Diam 2 in/5.1 cm.

Two-Mold Glass Bottles in Cabinet

14. BROWN CYLINDRICAL BOTTLE

Marked "P U G 55/1945." About 1910.

H 5 in/12.8 cm; Diam 1¼ in/3.2 cm. J/G B (14–17)

15. BROWN OVAL BOTTLE

Marked "ROTH & CO./SAN FRANCISCO CAL./1224." Glass stopper with cork. About 1910.

H 6½ in/16.6 cm; W 3 in/7.6 cm; D 1⅛ in/2.9 cm.

16. CLEAR RECTANGULAR BOTTLE

Marked "Chas. H. Fletcher's CASTORIA." About 1910.

H 5¾ in/14.7 cm; W 1⅞ in/4.9 cm; D 1 in/2.6 cm.

17. CLEAR OVAL BOTTLE

Recessed panel for paper label. About 1910.

H 6 in/5.2 cm; W 2¼ in/5.6 cm; D 1 3/16/3 cm.

18. RAG RUG

This rug was made about 1935 by Edith Stock Stewart, the lender's mother, from scraps of cotton cloth used on the 96 Ranch.

L 50 in/127 cm; W 35 in/88.9 cm. L/M S

19. QUILTED COVERLET

This coverlet was made in the "double wedding ring" pattern by Catherine Stewart, the lender's grandmother, from pieced cotton scraps found about 1930 on the 96 Ranch.

L and W 60 in/152.4 cm. L/M S

20. SAMPLE QUILT

This quilt was made by Viola or Frances Case about 1920 from samples of men's suiting that their father, J. B. Case, sold at his mercantile store in Paradise Valley.

L 69 in/174.2 cm; W 49 in/124.5 cm. J/G B

20

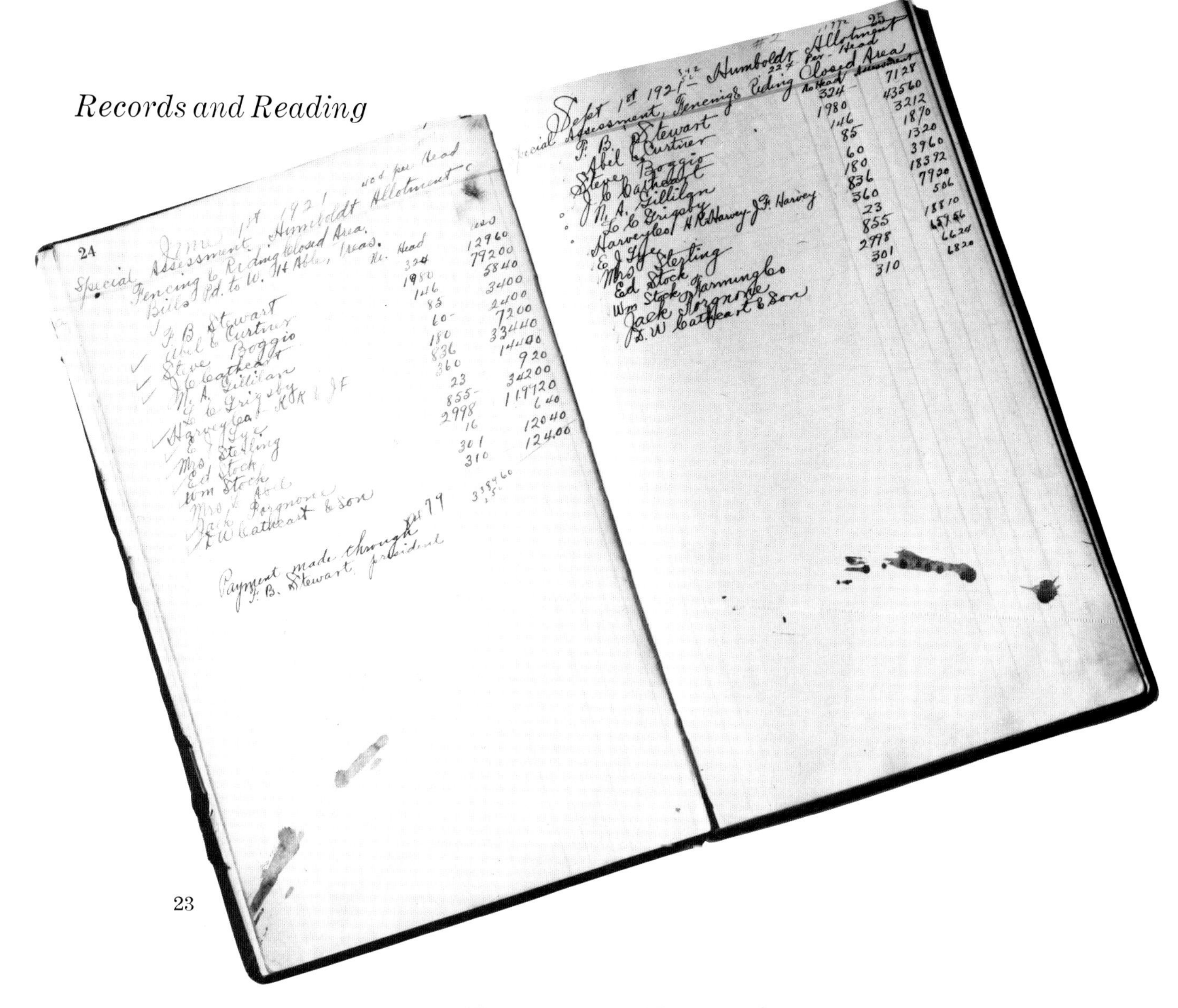

23

21. A FAMILY BIBLE

Published by John Winston, Philadelphia, in 1905, the "Christian Workers Holy Bible" records four generations of the Stock/Stewart family in Paradise Valley.

H 9¼ in/23.5 cm; W 6½ in/16.5 cm; D 1¾ in/4.5 cm. L/M S

22. A FAMILY PHOTO ALBUM

This commercial product of the 1880s is a typical Victorian-era object to be displayed in the parlor, to provide discrete entertainment, and to portray the family structure.

H 11¾ in/29.8 cm; W 9¼ in/23.5 cm; D 2¼ in/5.7 cm. L/M S

26

23. CATTLEMEN'S LEDGER

Used from 1905 into the 1930s by the Paradise Valley Cattle Growers Protective Association, the book is a typical document of self-interest groups in the West.

H 14 in/35.6 cm; W 8¾ in/22.2 cm; D ¾ in/1.9 cm. J/G B

24-26. AMERICAN MAGAZINES

The *Farm Journal* (1906), *Ladies' World* (1907), and *Saturday Evening Post* (1929) exemplified the useful, stylish, and popular magazines that found their way to the ranching frontier.

Hs 12 in/30.5 cm, 11¼ in/28.6 cm, 11 in/28 cm; Ws 9 in/22.9 cm, 16 in/40.6 cm, 16 in/40.6 cm. J/G B

27, 28. SCHOOLGIRL COOKBOOKS

Made from school "composition books" in 1905 and 1910 by Viola C. Case, aunt of the lender, and Mrs. J. W. Baker, both of whom recorded local recipes.

H 8¼ in/21 cm; W 7 in/17.8 cm. J/G B

29, 30. BEER BOTTLES

Beer was shipped to Nevada from Germany, the homeland of some of its settlers, in high-fired ceramic bottles by 1900. Most American firms preferred molded glass.

Hs 8½ in/21.6 cm, 11½ in/29.2 cm; Diams 3 in/7.6 cm. L/M S, PP

31. WINE CASK

Made of oak about 1920 and marked "SIERRA WINE AND LIQUOR CO./RENO, NEVADA." California wine began to compete with home production as income rose and tastes changed.

H 26 in/66 cm; Diam 16 in/40.7 cm (NMHT-EI 1979.0254.16).

32. MIXER

This factory-made "egg beater" is marked "AJ" in diamond, "Made in USA/Pat. Oct. 9, 1923." It was considered a symbol of progress and modernization in the ranch kitchen.

L 11 in/28 cm. J/G B

33. COFFEE CAN

This 2½ pound, tinned zinc can is marked "Folger's Golden Gate/Steel cut coffee" for regional appeal. About 1930.

H 8¼/21 cm; Diam 5 in/12.7 cm. J/G B

34, 35. CHINESE GLAZED EARTHENWARE

The spouted soy sauce jug and the flared-mouth wine jar, imported between 1870 and 1910, reflect the presence of Chinese laborers on the Central Pacific Railroad and in local mines and shops.

Hs 4½ in/11.4 cm, 4 in/10.2 cm; Diams 4 in/10.2 cm, 3 in/7.6 cm (NMHT-CG 1979.0254.3 and 4).

27

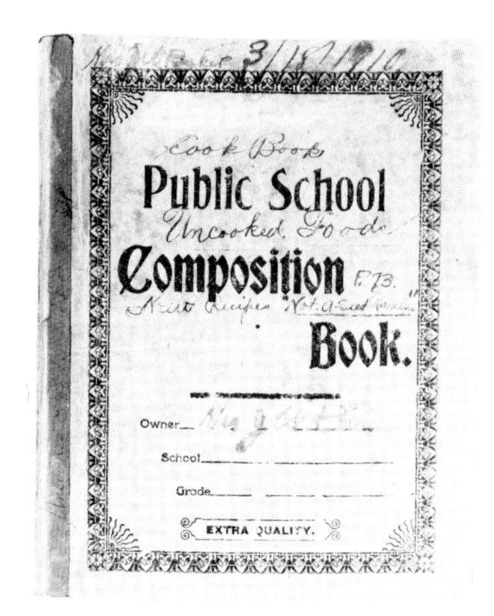

28

34

37

Costume

36. CUFFS

Commercially made about 1920 from leather and brass, the pair were used by the lender's uncle, Bill, to protect his shirt and wrists and for display.

L 6¾ in/17.1 cm; Diams 3 in/7.6 cm, 4¼ in/10.8 cm. AM

37. HAIR CHAPS

About 1920, Gerhard Miller, Jr., the lender's father, bought this pair of Angora goat hide chaps, marked "J. M. Capriola, Maker/Elko, Nevada." The name, *chaparreras*, and use of these leather leg protectors comes from Hispanic Mexico.

L 38½ in/97.8 cm; Leg W 13½ in/ 34.3 cm. AM

38. ITALIAN SWEATER

About 1938, Silvia Forgnone, the lender's aunt in his hometown of Passo Breve in northwestern Italy, knitted this sweater as a gift for him.

L 23⅝ in/60 cm; Underarm W 16 in/ 40.6 cm. J/G B

39. GLOVES

The pair was made of tanned deerhide about 1940 by Harvey Cracker on the Boggio's Sperry Ranch.

L 8 in/20.3 cm; W 4½ in/11.4 cm. J/G B

40. "COWBOY BOOT" SHOES

About 1935, Steve Boggio, the lender's father, bought this pair for special occasions. Note the stitching on the squared toe and the undercut heels.

L 11 in/28 cm; H 7 in/17.8 cm; W 3⅞/9.8 cm. J/G B

41. TWO-PIECE SUIT

Made of striped worsted about 1935, this up-to-date, ready-made suit was available through mail order catalogues and local stores.

Trouser waist 28 in/71.1 cm; inseam 27 in/ 68.6 cm; coat back L 28 in/71.1 cm; shoulder W 16 in/40.6 cm; sleeve L 24 in/61 cm. PP

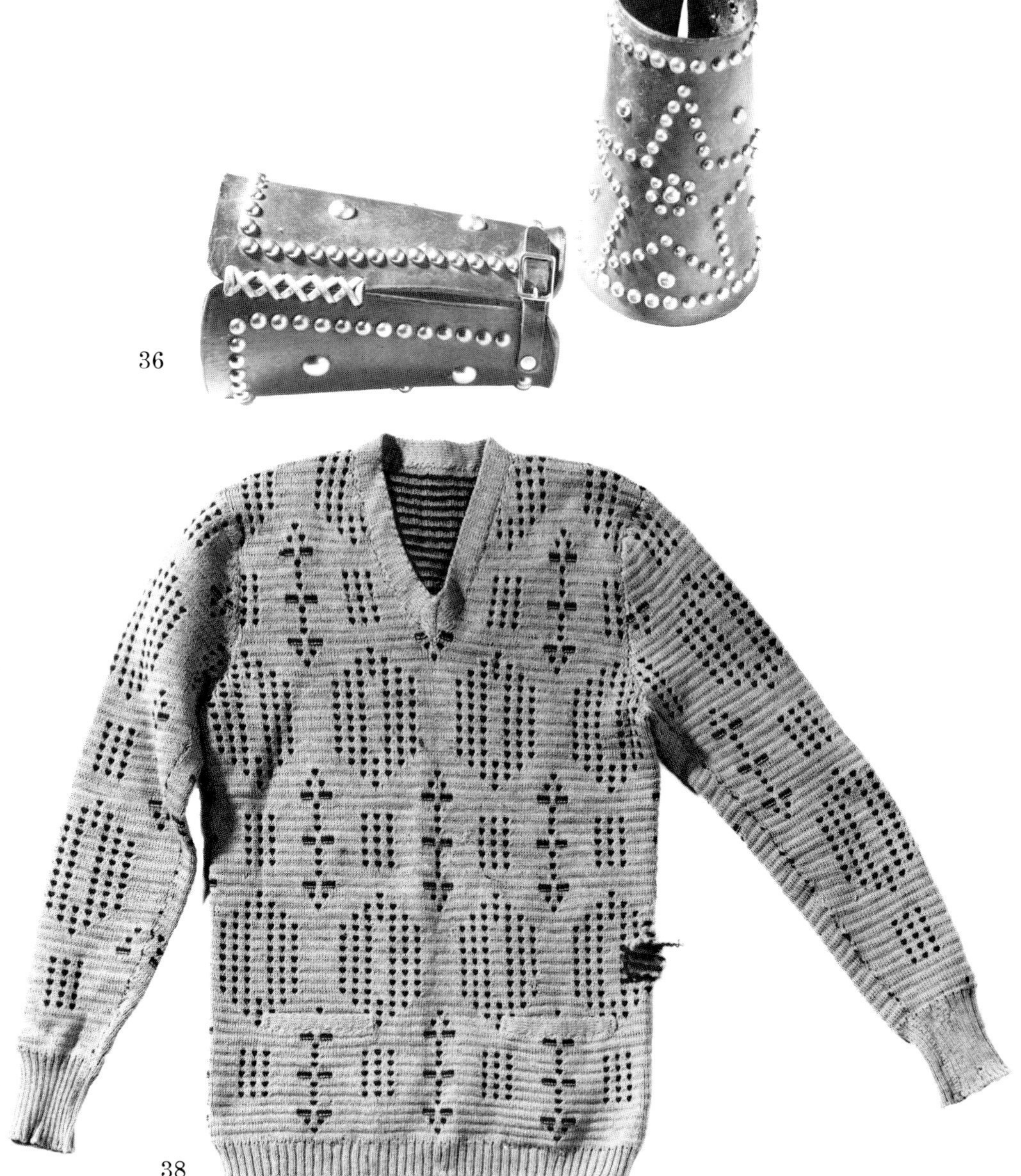

36

38

39

Tools and Crafts

Buckaroo tools and crafts reflect a way of life and, in effect, make it possible.

The buckaroo must possess many skills as part of his life on horseback. Although very few buckaroos make stock saddles or pack saddle gear, they repair these items and make secondary saddlery equipment.

Buckaroos may be "rawhiders," making lariats, hackamores, quirts, and bosals, with special tools. They also work tanned leather into knife scabbards, belts, and taps. After being twisted with a rotating device, horsehair is braided into ropes called macardies.

Pete Pedroli says, "Hell, every buckaroo is half blacksmith." Horseshoeing equipment is as familiar to buckaroos as branding irons. In his spare time, a buckaroo may turn out a few spurs or bits, using patterns and parts from catalogues or his imagination.

One-of-a-kind, hand-crafted products also reflect the cowboy's work, time off, and inventiveness. Some tools are not very popular with buckaroos, such as those used to cut and store wood, to fix fences or ditches, or to hook, shear, and brand sheep.

Saddlery

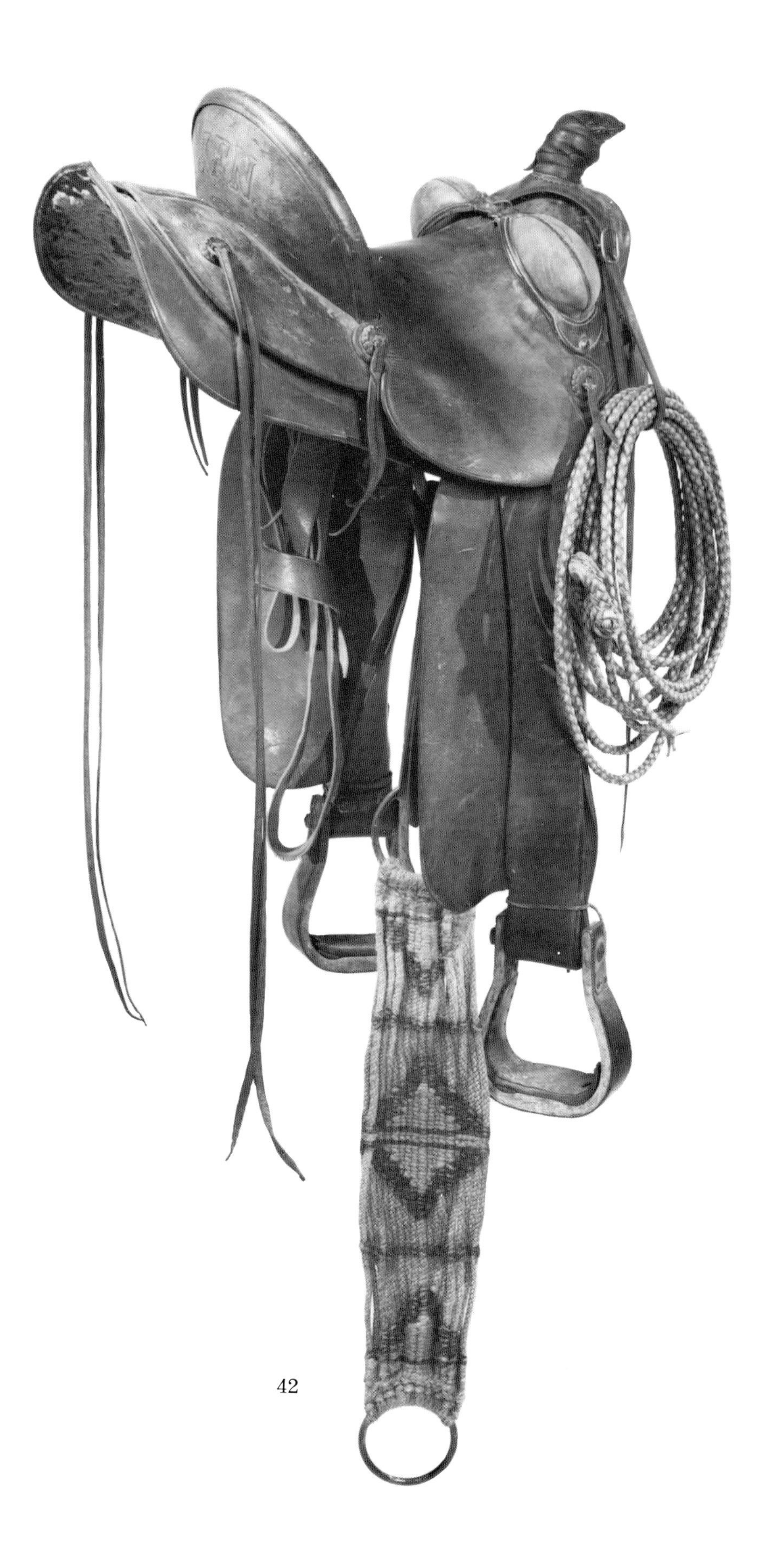

42

42. STOCK SADDLE

This saddle was made about 1930 in California by the "Visalia Stock Saddle Company, #28089." Many Nevada buckaroos preferred its features: one centrally placed cinch (center-fired, single-rigged) and an unswelled pommel (slick fork) with bucking rolls.

Tree seat L 14½ in/36.8 cm; cantle W 13 in/33 cm. AM

43. BUCKING ROLLS

This device helped hold the rider's legs in place (see item 42). This pair is a factory product of about 1950.

Single: L 9 in/22.9 cm; H and W 3½ in/8.9 cm. L/M S

44. OREGON SHORT LINE

This device was attached under the horse's belly to the inner face of both stirrups to keep them down during rough rides.

L 19 in/48.3 cm; W 1³/₁₆ in/3 cm. L/M S

45. SADDLE BLANKET

Machine-woven about 1950 in a plaid design, the blanket was placed under the saddle to cushion the horse's withers and haunches and to soak up sweat.

L 58 in/147.3 cm; W 29 in/73.7 cm. L/M S

46. STOCK SADDLE

Probably made in Wyoming about 1950, this typical ranch saddle displays a swelled pommel. Like item 42, it is made from a wooden tree, leather coverings and rosettes, and iron D rings holding the single cotton cinch. The horn is wrapped to protect it and to ease the run of the rope.

Tree: seat L 14 in/35.6 cm; W 13¾ in/34.4 cm. L/M S

47. PACK SADDLE WITH FULL RIGGING

Even after pickup trucks changed ranch life (about 1950), pack animals continued to haul supplies into the back country. This type is called a "saw buck"; it is a factory product of about 1960.

L 20 in/50.8 cm; H 9 in/22.9 cm; W 16 in/40.7 cm. L/M S

48. PACK SADDLE PAD

Canvas is stitched to a horsehair pad to make a protective blanket under the heavy pack saddle. About 1950.

L 29 in/73.7 cm; W 28 in/71.1 cm. L/M S

OVERLEAF:

Myron Smart and Les Stewart catch horses to saddle for work at the Black Ridge line camp.

49. PACK COVER

Made about 1950 of heavy canvas with ten metal eyes for tie-down ropes.

L 76½ in/194.3 cm; W 61½ in/ 156.2 cm. L/M S

50. LASH CINCH WITH ROPE

This special strap goes over the top of the pack load. It was factory made about 1960.

L 29½ in/74.4 cm; W 4 in/10.1 cm. L/M S

51. PACK SADDLE BAGS

Commercial products of heavy canvas, wood, and leather, made about 1950 and marked for the 96 Ranch. One is hung from each side of the pack saddle before the upper load is placed.

H and W 26 in/66 cm; D (empty) 1 in/2.5 cm. L/M S

52. HALTER AND LEAD LINE

Machine-made objects of leather straps, metal rings, and braided cotton, used to lead pack animals. About 1950.

Center strap L 14½ in/36.2 cm; Line L 75 in/190.6 cm. L/M S

53. HOBBLES

On the range, this commercial object is fastened to the front legs of an animal likely to wander off. About 1950.

L 15 in/38.1 cm; Cuff W and Diam 3 in/7.6 cm. PP

54, 55. NECK STRAP WITH BELL

These machine-made products were hung on a trained "bell" mule or mare and the chain end linked to a rope for securing an animal. The strap is carved with "PEDROLI" and the "Bell-T" brand. About 1950.

Strap L 30 in/76.2 cm; W 2½ in/ 6.4 cm; Bell H 7 in/17.8 cm; W 5 in/ 12.7 cm; D 2¾ in/ 7 cm. PP

56, 57. CURRY COMB AND BRUSH

These commercial objects are the basic tools used to groom a horse's coat. About 1960.

Comb L 8¾ in/22.2 cm; W 4 in/ 10.2 cm; H 1¾ in/4.5 cm; Brush L 8¼/21 cm; W 2¾ in/7 cm; H 3 in/ 7.6 cm. L/M S

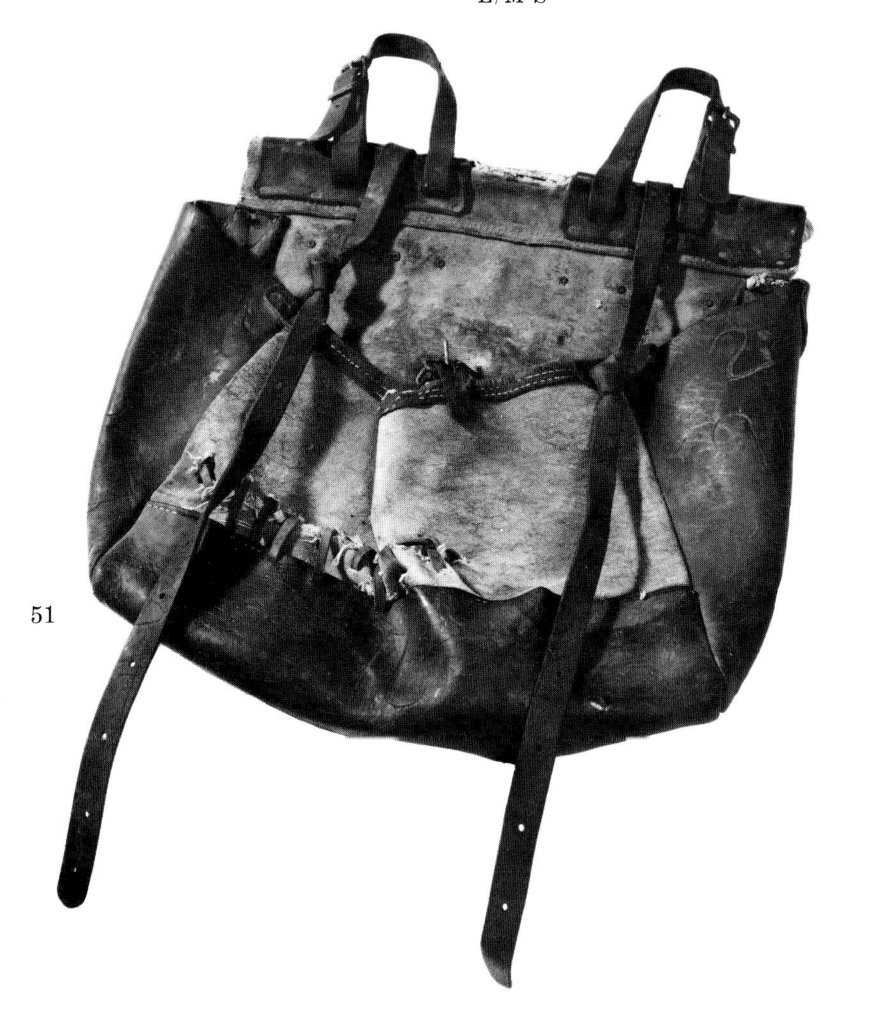

51

54, 55

Leather, Hair, and Rawhide Work

58. STITCHING BENCH

Also called a harness horse, this factory product served since about 1950 as a seat and a clamp to hold saddlery leather for sewing.

H 40 in/101.6 cm; Seat H 24⅛ in/ 61.3 cm; L 31½ in/80 cm; W 11⅝ in/ 29.5 cm. AM

59, 60. POCKET KNIFE AND SCABBARD

In 1978 buckaroo Chuck Wheelock made the scabbard for the lender's "Buck" pocket knife. Such "Stockman" knives are used for making leather thongs and in other work, like ear notching.

Knife L 3⅞ in/9.8 cm; Scabbard Strap L 8½ in/ 21.6 cm; Scabbard L 3½ in/ 8.9 cm; W 1⅝ in/4.1 cm. HM

61, 62. LEATHER-TRIMMING GAUGES

Locally made about 1950, these blocks, with a pocket knife (item 59) inserted into the tinned notch, could trim irregular strips of rawhide into even-width, beveled thongs for braided lariats, hackamores, and quirts.

Ls 10 in/25.4 cm, 8 in/20.3 cm; Hs 3 in/7.6 cm; Ds 2 in/5.1 cm, 1½ in/3.8 cm (NMHT-CL 1979.0253.02 and 3). L/M S

63, 64, 65. LEATHER-WORK NEEDLES

Also known as marlinespikes, they are used to work rawhide into braiding. Item 63 is a handmade awl from about 1940.

63 L 6 in/15.2 cm; W 1¼ in/3.2 cm; 64 and 65 Ls 7 in/17.8 cm (NMHT-CL 1979.0254.04 and 5). PP, L/M S

66. BOSAL

The term is used for a small braided rawhide hackamore. With a leather thong attached, it becomes a lightweight halter.

H 11 in/27.9 cm; W 7½ in/17 cm. L/M S

59, 60

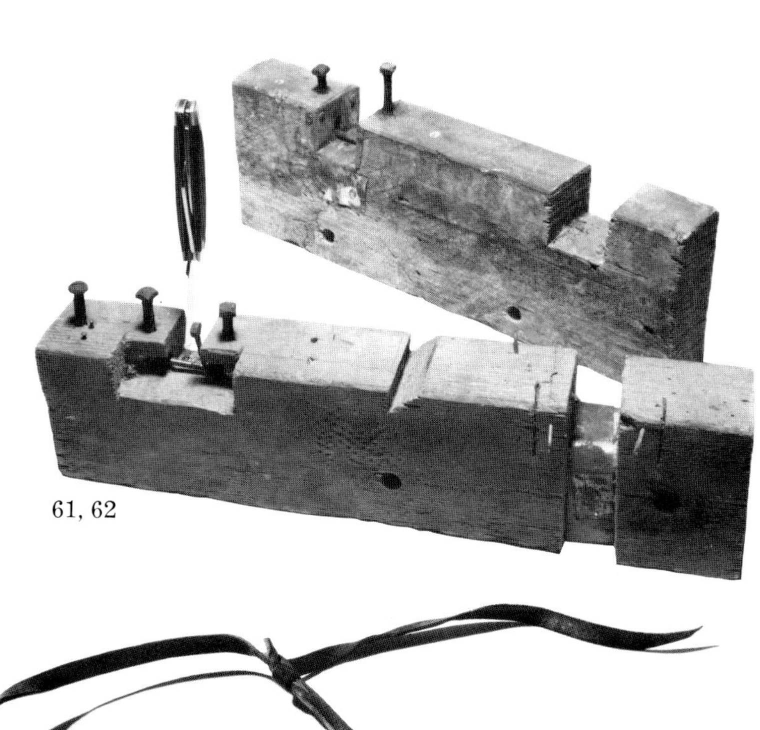

61, 62

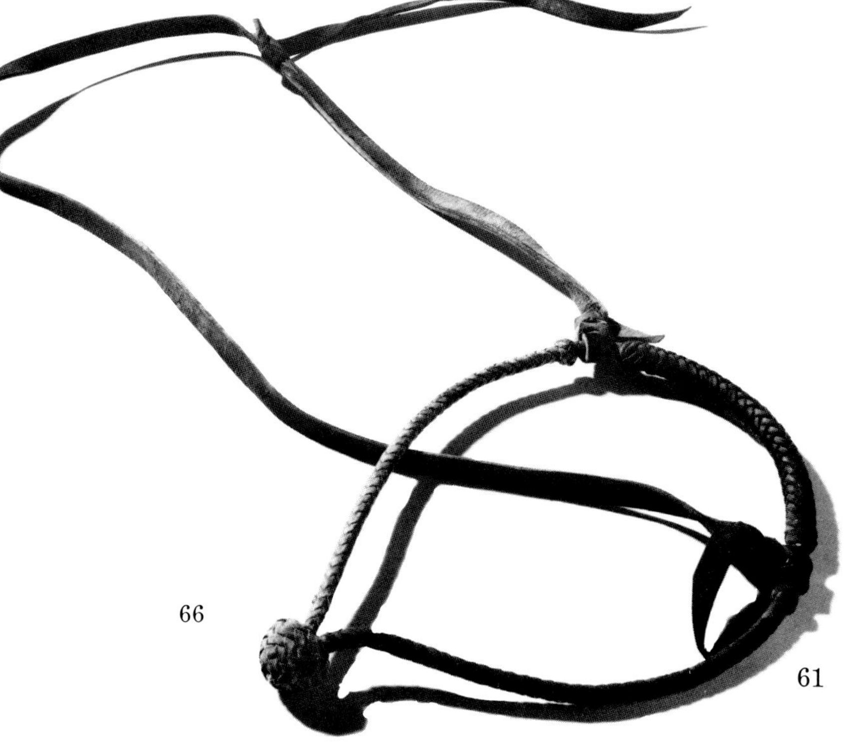

66

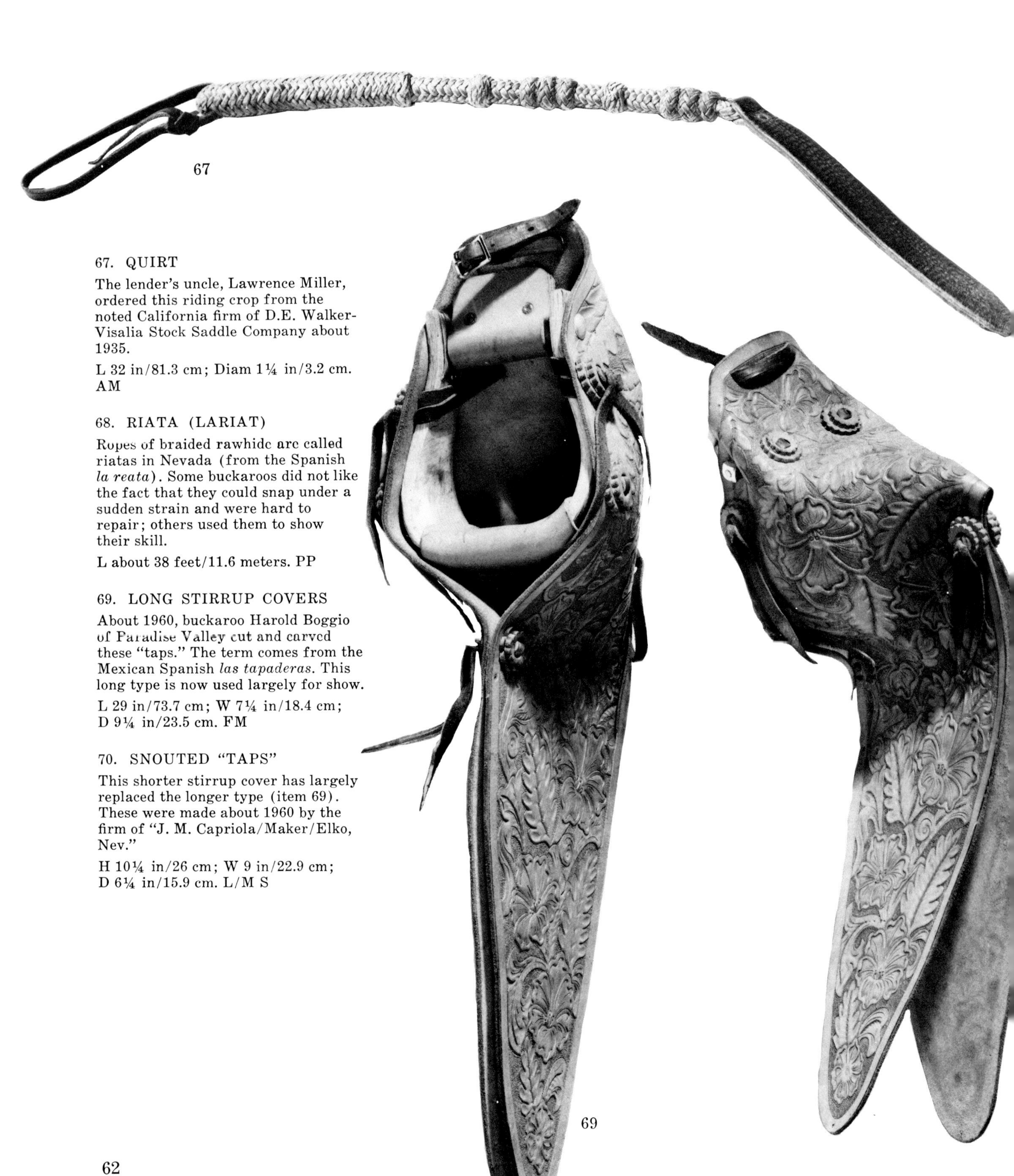

67

69

67. QUIRT

The lender's uncle, Lawrence Miller, ordered this riding crop from the noted California firm of D.E. Walker-Visalia Stock Saddle Company about 1935.

L 32 in/81.3 cm; Diam 1¼ in/3.2 cm. AM

68. RIATA (LARIAT)

Ropes of braided rawhide are called riatas in Nevada (from the Spanish *la reata*). Some buckaroos did not like the fact that they could snap under a sudden strain and were hard to repair; others used them to show their skill.

L about 38 feet/11.6 meters. PP

69. LONG STIRRUP COVERS

About 1960, buckaroo Harold Boggio of Paradise Valley cut and carved these "taps." The term comes from the Mexican Spanish *las tapaderas*. This long type is now used largely for show.

L 29 in/73.7 cm; W 7¼ in/18.4 cm; D 9¼ in/23.5 cm. FM

70. SNOUTED "TAPS"

This shorter stirrup cover has largely replaced the longer type (item 69). These were made about 1960 by the firm of "J. M. Capriola/Maker/Elko, Nev."

H 10¼ in/26 cm; W 9 in/22.9 cm; D 6¼ in/15.9 cm. L/M S

71. HAIR TWISTER

Made of pine in 1978 by the donor, "LJS," this traditional Mexican-Spanish *tarabilla* twists horsetail hair into a cord when the block is rotated on the spindle. The cord is braided or twisted into a rope (item 72). A videotape of the process is preserved in the Library of Congress's American Folklife Center.

Block L 10 in/25.4 cm; W and D 1½ in/3.8 cm; Spindle L 12½ in/31.8 cm (NMHT-CL 1979.0253.01). L/M S

72. HAIR ROPE OR MACARDY

The twisted horsetail hair rope is locally called a "macardy," from the Mexican-Spanish *mecate*, for maguey-fiber rope. This example was made about 1930 at the State Prison in Carson City.

L 19 ft 1 in/5.82 m; Diam ½ in/1.3 cm. J/G B

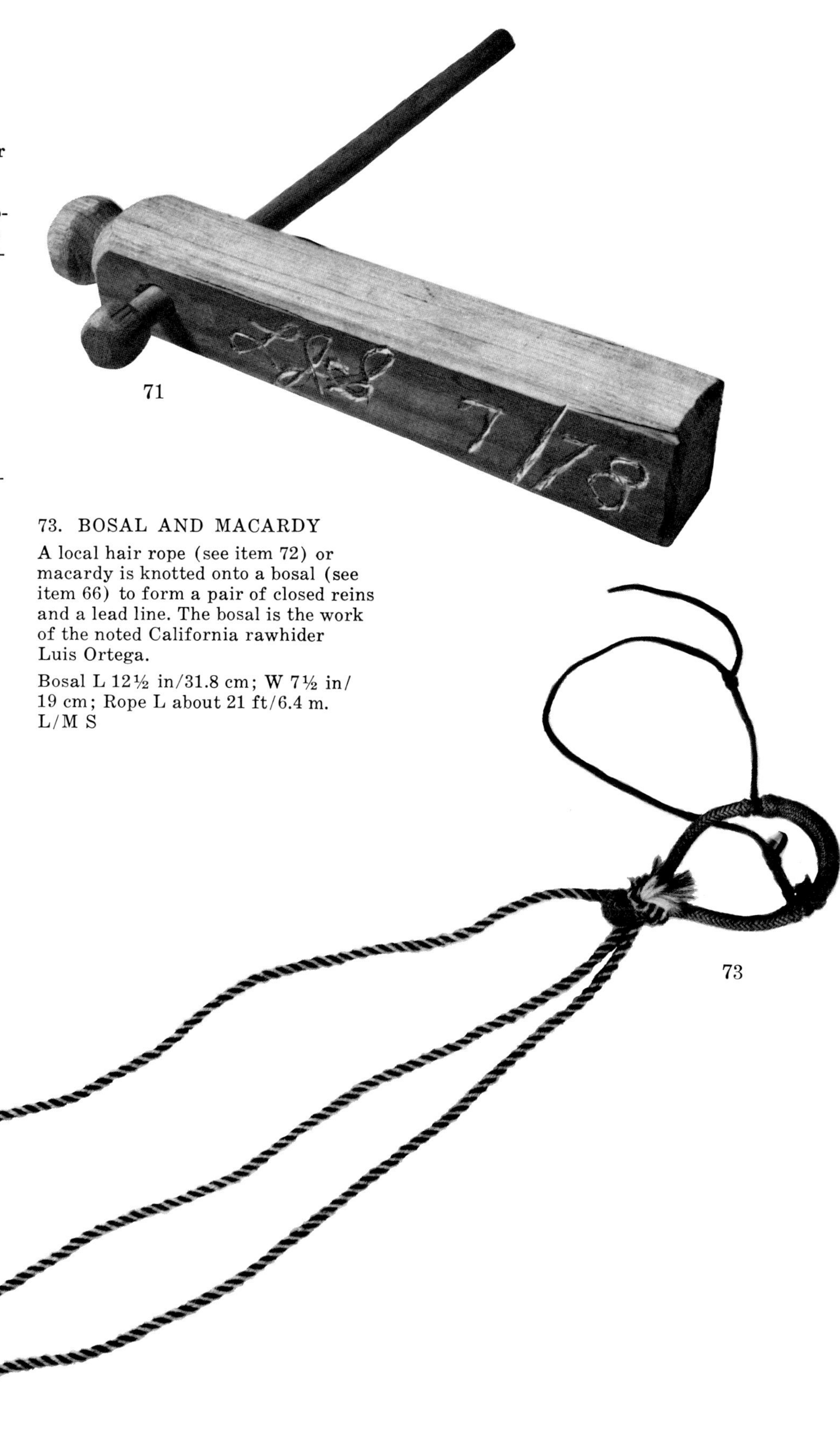

71

73. BOSAL AND MACARDY

A local hair rope (see item 72) or macardy is knotted onto a bosal (see item 66) to form a pair of closed reins and a lead line. The bosal is the work of the noted California rawhider Luis Ortega.

Bosal L 12½ in/31.8 cm; W 7½ in/19 cm; Rope L about 21 ft/6.4 m. L/M S

73

Blacksmithing

74. TOOLBOX FOR HORSESHOEING

The sturdy, local box contains some medicines (items 88-90) and tools (items 75-86) used for the never-ending task of shoeing horses.

L 23 in/58.4 cm; H 8 in/20.3 cm; D. 12 in/30.5 cm. L/M S (74-90)

75. RASP

Marked "Cleancut" and "96," the rasp is used to smooth the hoof before nailing on the shoe.

L 18½ in/47 cm; W 1⅞ in/4.7 cm.

76. RASP

This item is marked "NICHOLSON" and protected in a leather sheath. About 1950.

L 17⅝ in/44.8 cm; W 1¾ in/4.4 cm.

77. BOX FOR HORSESHOE NAILS

"Capewell" box for standard 2-inch nails. About 1970.

L 8½ in/21.6 cm; H 2 in/5.1 cm; W 4¼ in/10.8 cm.

78, 79. HORSESHOES

Six new and used horseshoes, marked "#F JAPAN."

L and W 5 in/12.7 cm.

74

87

80. ALLIGATOR PLIERS

This device is used for clinching off nails in hoof. About 1950.

L 13¼ in/33.7 cm; W 1¼ in/3.2 cm; D ¾ in/1.9 cm.

81. HOOF PARER

Marked "96" for the Stewart ranch and "HELLER . . . U.S.A." for the manufacturer, these tools are used to pull off shoes and trim hooves. About 1950.

L 14⅜ in/36.5 cm; W 3½ in/8.9 cm; D 1⅛ in/2.9 cm.

82. HOOF PARER

This parer, with set-screw jaws (one missing), is marked "OUR PRIDE CHANNELLOCK." About 1960.

L 13⅞ in/35.3 cm; W 3 in/7.6 cm; D 1 in/2.6 cm.

83. HOOF PARER

Marked "DASCO HOOF PARER." About 1950.

L 14¼ in/36.2 cm; W 2¾ in/7 cm; D ¾ in/1.9 cm.

82

84. CHISEL

Marked "STANLEY ALLOY/ ¾ / . . . USA." Used to cut heels off of horseshoes.

L 7⅛ in/8.2 cm; W ¾ in/1.9 cm.

85. HOOF KNIFE

Made about 1960, the hooked blade set in a bone haft is marked "WADE BUTCHER/SHEFFIELD/ENGLAND." It is used to clean out the frog of the hoof.

L 8 in/20.3 cm; W 1 in/2.6 cm.

86. HORSESHOEING HAMMER

This is a specialized, claw-type hammer.

L 14 in/35.6 cm; Head L 4 in/10.2 cm; W ⅞ in/2.3 cm.

87. ANVIL

Section cut from an iron railroad rail. About 1960.

L 14 in/35.6 cm; H 6 in/15.2 cm; W 5½ in/14 cm.

88. "ABSORBINE FLYCHEX" MEDICINE

This tin can contains a fly protectant for horses. About 1970.

H 6¼ in/5.9 cm; W 3⅞ in/9.9 cm; D 1¾ in/4.5 cm.

89. "SULFAREKA" MEDICINE

This plastic bottle contains a powder for animal wounds. About 1970.

H 5¾ in/14.6 cm; Diam 2 in/5.1 cm.

90. "SPOHN'S COMPOUND" MEDICINE

This glass bottle contains an animal expectorant. About 1970.

H 5¼ in/13.3 cm; W 2⅜ in/6 cm; D 1½ in/ 3.8 cm.

91. TONGS

These long-snouted iron devices are used by blacksmiths to hold pieces in the making.

L 23¾ in/60.3 cm; W 3⅜ in/8.6 cm; D 1⅝ in/ 4.1 cm (NMHT-CL 1979.0254.01).

92. TONGS

These display a shorter jaw than item 91, and were also acquired in northern Nevada. Both date to about 1960.

L 18½ in/40.7 cm; (NMHT-CL 1979.0254.02).

Other Buckaroo Tools

93. HUNTING KNIFE AND SCABBARD

Marked "MARBLE/GLADSTONE/MICH./ PAT.D 1918(?)" on the knife and "JB/ 1930" on the sheath, this item was used for many purposes by the buckaroo.

Knife L 8¼ in/21 cm; W 1¼ in/ 3.2 cm; D ⅞ in/ 2.2 cm. J/G B

94. HORSE CASTRATOR

Buckaroos had various reasons for neutering bulls and stallions. This hand-made device of leather and oak held the sperm ducts while the testes were cut free. About 1925.

L 10½ in/26.6 cm; W 2¼ in/5.7 cm; D ¾ in/1.9 cm. J/G B

93

95, 96. HAYING HOOKS

Earlier (1930?) and later (1960?) examples of the tools used to handle the bulky bales of hay.

Ls 9½ in/24.1 cm, 7½ in/19 cm (wood handle); Ws 4½ in/11.4 cm, 4⅝ in/11.7 cm. PP

97. TRIVET

A hand-wrought iron device found near Hartscrabble, a quartz refining site in the valley. It may have held a smelting pot with many smaller crucibles. Some buckaroos tried prospecting in the area.

H 2¾ in/7 cm; Diam 6½ in/16.5 cm (NMHT-CL 1980.0019.02).

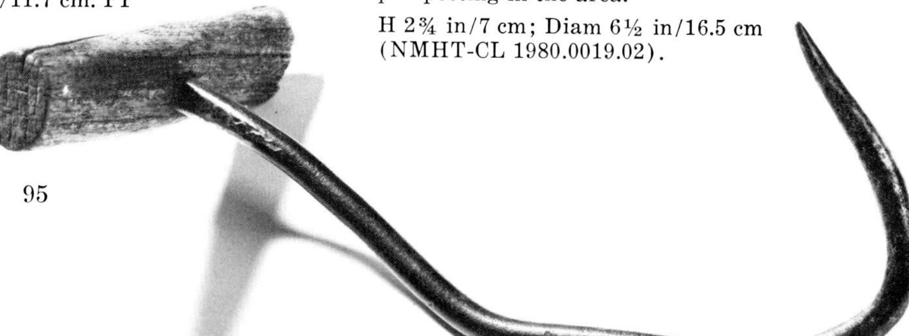

95

Branding Irons

98–116. BRANDING IRONS

The branding iron is an important product of western blacksmithing. When heated, it burns the owner's mark or brand on the hide of the cattle. Because some irons are similar, ear notches and throat wattles are also cut onto the cattle to aid in identification. Rights to use a certain brand or iron may be sold separately from ranch property. Branding irons came from Hispanic Mexico, where they developed before 1600. Hinged-handle irons and small pieces called "running-irons" are packed behind the saddle and used in open-range branding. Each iron is the creation of an individual blacksmith-buckaroo.

99

98

98. BULL HEAD IRON

This iron was first recorded in 1884 by Jason Farrel of Paradise Valley. It was next used by the Jordan Valley Stock Co. until 1915, when it went to the Blisses in Golconda.

L (broken) 10 in/25.4 cm; Head H 6 in/15.2 cm, W 5 in/12.7 cm. PP (98-108)

99. P BENCH IRON

Similar brands appear in Elko in 1872 and later in Reno.

L (cut) 21¾ in/55.2 cm; Head H 5 in/12.7 cm, W 3 in/7.6 cm.

100. C REVERSE S IRON

The iron was first recorded by George D. Bliss of Golconda in 1885 and eventually traded in 1946 to the Bull Head Cattle Co. of Winnemucca and Reno. Originally, the *S* was not reversed. This iron is hinged to make it easier to pack.

L (open) 24⅞ in/63.2 cm; Head H 3½ in/8.9 cm, W 5¼ in/13.3 cm.

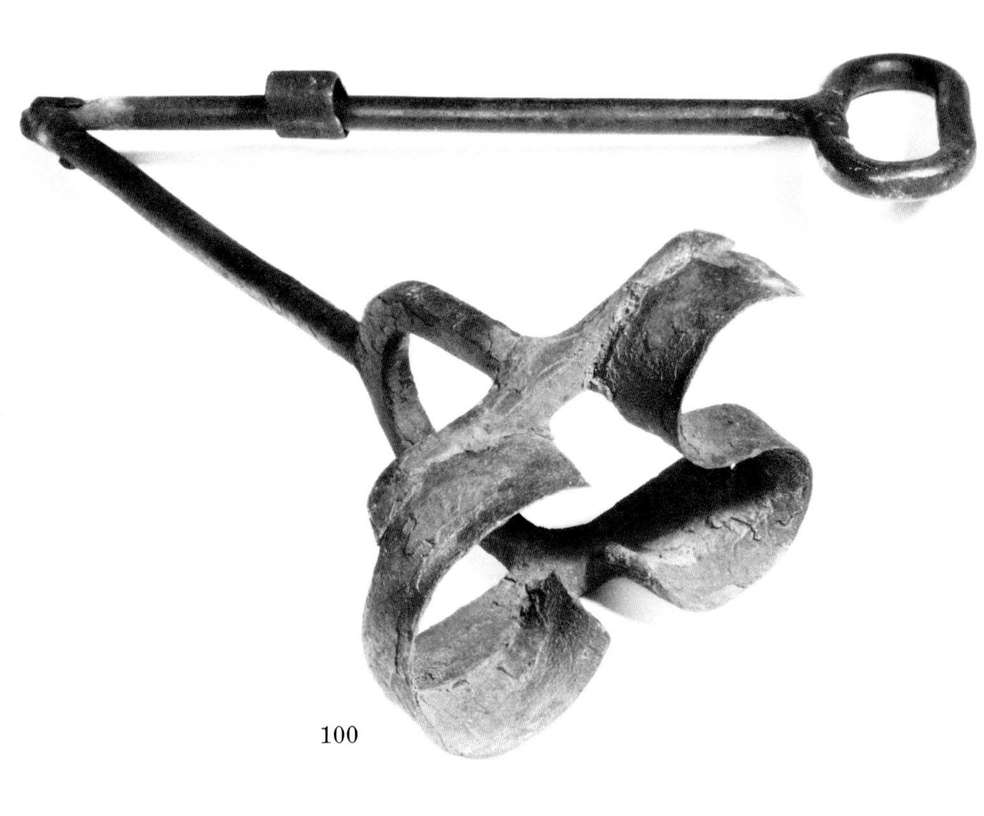

100

101. QUARTER CIRCLE A IRON

The iron was first recorded by Abel and Curtner of Willow Point; it was traded to Winnemucca firms after 1940, when it was used only on cattle.

L 36⅜ in/92.4 cm; Head H 6 in/15.2 cm, W 7¾ in/19.7 cm.

102. DOUBLE SQUARE IRON

The horizontal version was recorded as a trade in 1909 from I. V. Button to John G. Taylor and Jason Edson, all of Winnemucca; later it was traded to a Clover Valley firm, "lost" in 1936, then located and used by F. E. Gorham only on horses, and finally traded into California.

L 31¾ in/80.6 cm; Head H 2¼ in/5.7 cm, W 4½ in/11.4 cm.

103. ROCKING CHAIR IRON

Used for cattle and horses, the iron was first recorded by Gerhard Miller, Sr., of Paradise Valley in 1886 and has remained with the family.

L 36 in/91.5 cm; Head H 4½ in/11.4 cm, W 4⅜ in/11.1 cm.

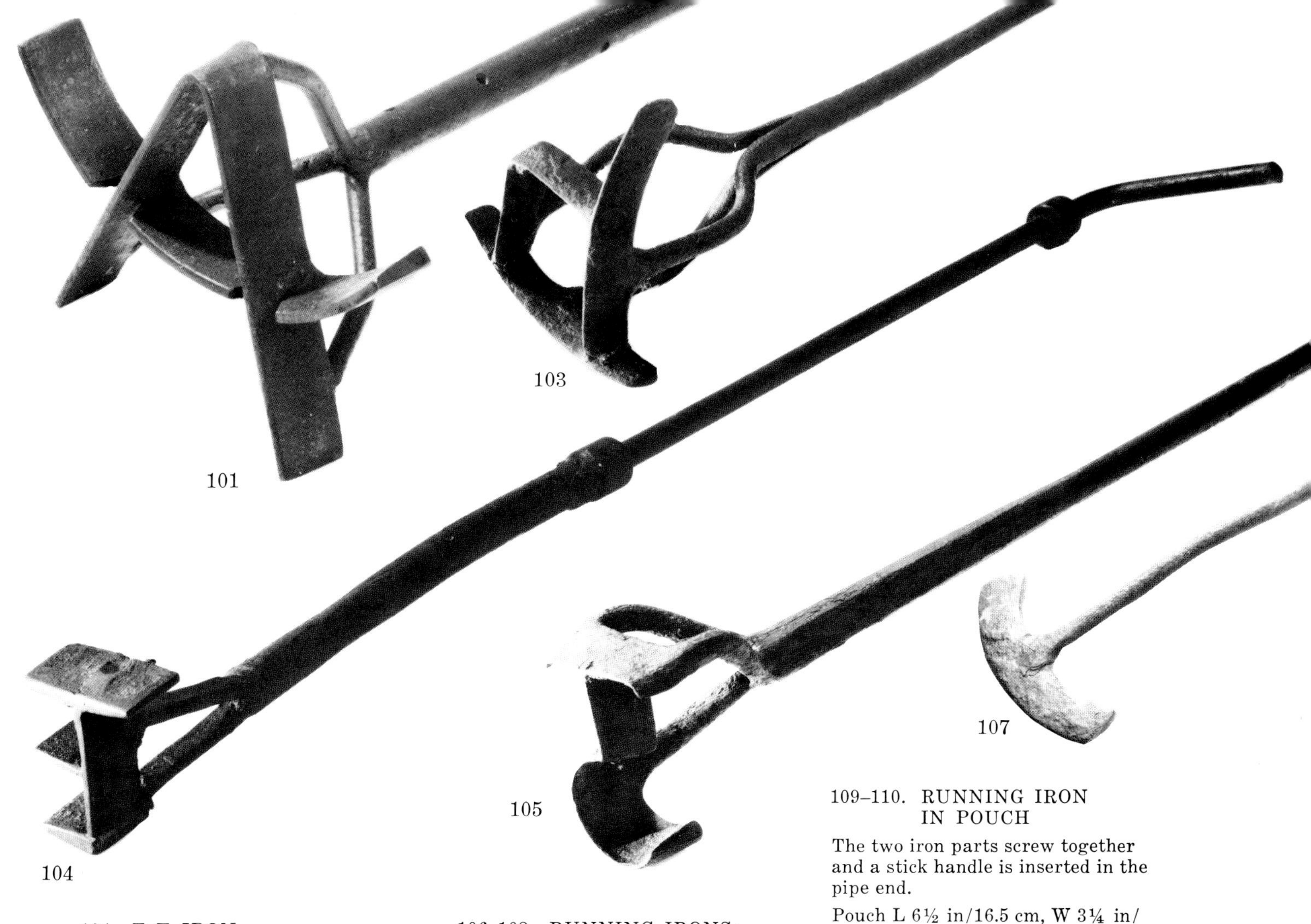

101

103

104

105

107

104. T E IRON

Used only on horses, the iron was first recorded by Abel and Curtner (see item 101) in 1916 and later traded to Winnemucca firms.

L 35¼ in/89.5 cm; Head H 2¼ in/5.7 cm, W 3 in/7.6 cm.

105. T 5 IRON

The iron was first recorded in Winnemucca by W. H. Holt in 1879 and used only on cattle. In 1916 John Forgnone of Paradise Valley recorded it for cattle and horses; by 1942 it was traded to local Basque ranchers Santiago, Fermin, Frank Gavica, and John and Delfina Zatica.

L 34⅝ in/88 cm; Head H 2⅜ in/6 cm, W 3 in/ 7.6 cm.

106–108. RUNNING IRONS: BAR, ARC, CIRCLE

Used to mark or alter brands, these irons are not recorded. The circle (item 108) is held in tension by two sticks.

106: L 27¾ in/70.5 cm, W 2 in/5.1 cm;

107: L 40 in/101.6 cm, W 5½ in/14 cm;

108: Diam 5½ in/14 cm.

109–110. RUNNING IRON IN POUCH

The two iron parts screw together and a stick handle is inserted in the pipe end.

Pouch L 6½ in/16.5 cm, W 3¼ in/8.2 cm; Iron L (together) 8¼ in/20.9 cm, W 1⅜ in/3.5 cm; Pipe (110 b) Diam ¾ in/1.9 cms (NMHT-CL 1980.0311.01 a, b and .04). W/I F

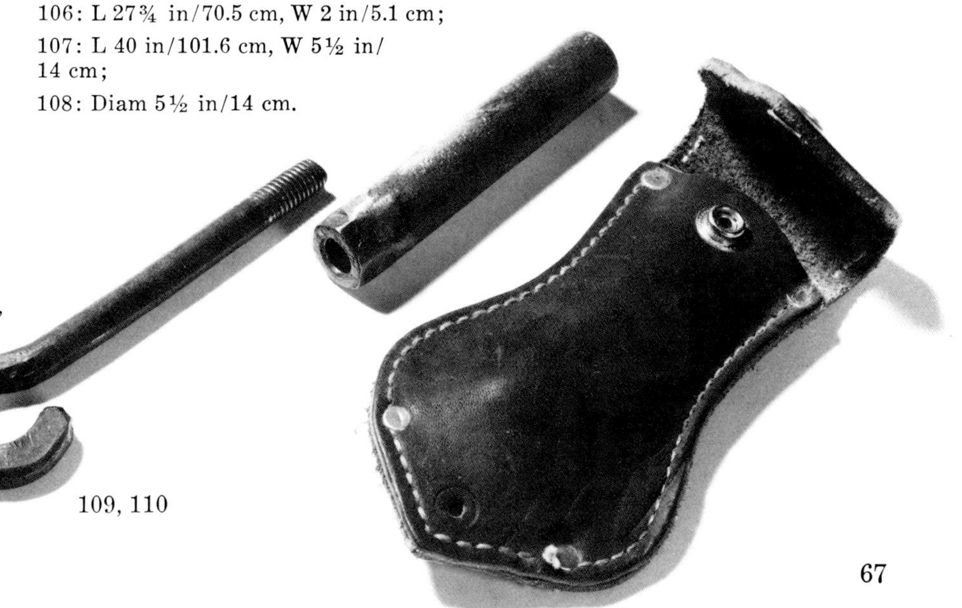

109, 110

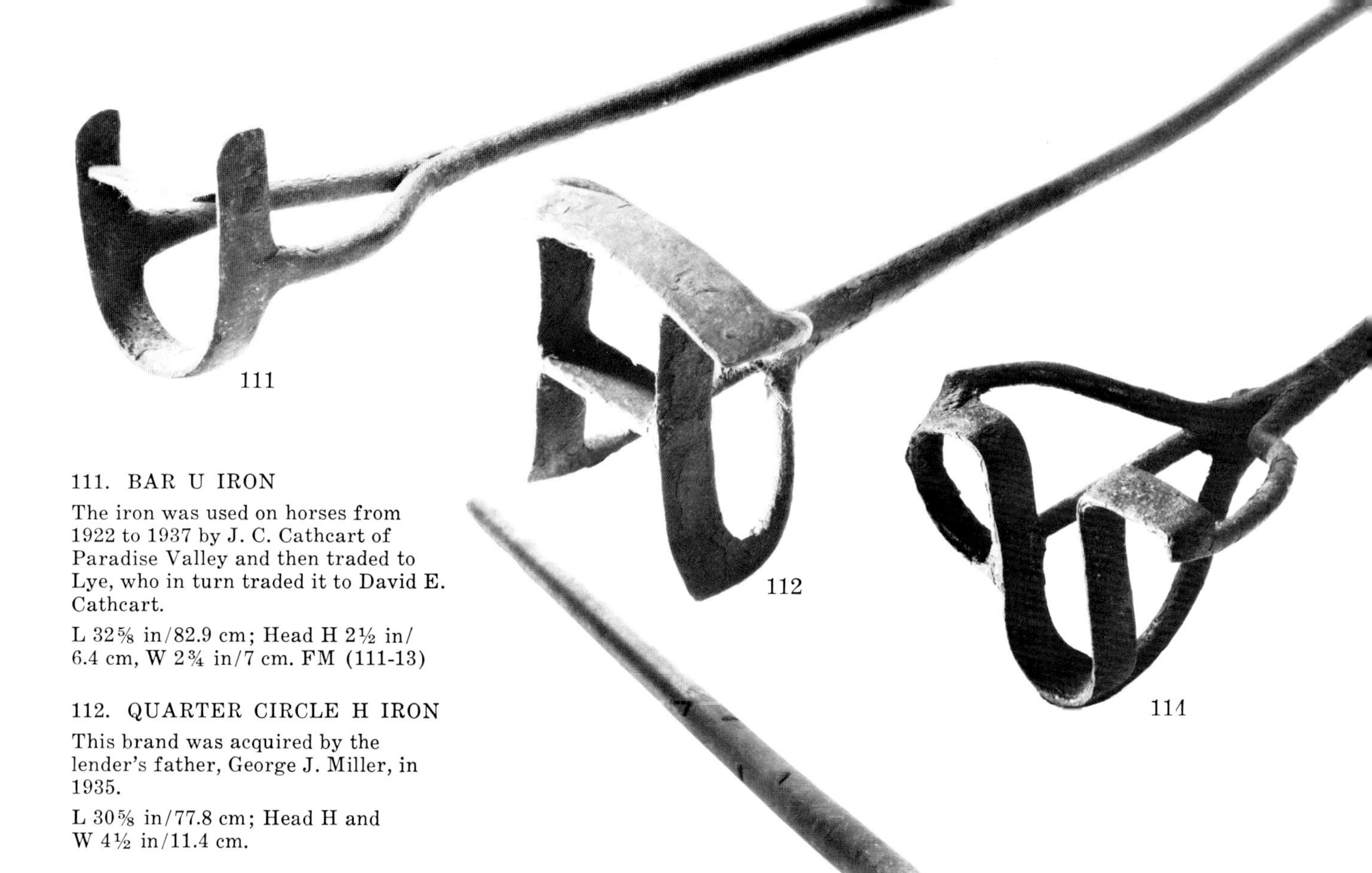

111. BAR U IRON

The iron was used on horses from 1922 to 1937 by J. C. Cathcart of Paradise Valley and then traded to Lye, who in turn traded it to David E. Cathcart.

L 32⅝ in/82.9 cm; Head H 2½ in/6.4 cm, W 2¾ in/7 cm. FM (111-13)

112. QUARTER CIRCLE H IRON

This brand was acquired by the lender's father, George J. Miller, in 1935.

L 30⅝ in/77.8 cm; Head H and W 4½ in/11.4 cm.

113. R O IRON

The iron was used only by Ottman Reil of Winnemucca beginning in 1895.

L 35 in/88.9 cm; Head H 3 in/7.6 cm, W 4½ in/11.4 cm.

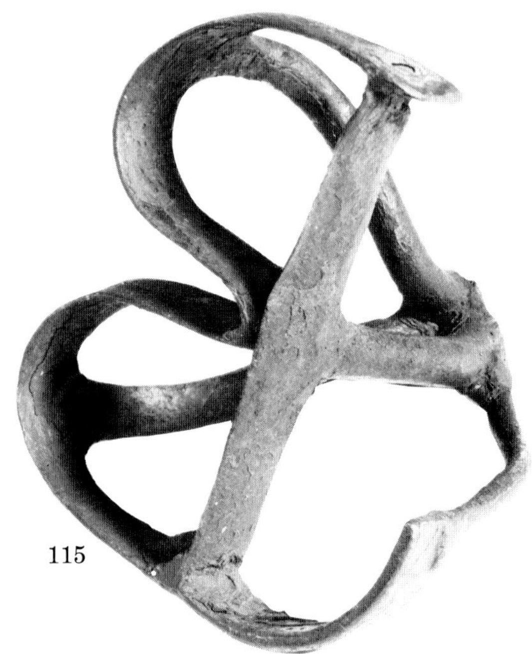

114. 7 U P IRON

The brand was first recorded in 1902 by Jason P. Byrnes of Paradise Valley, then in 1916 by Gideon Forgnone and Steve Boggio. This iron was made by blacksmith Seymour Riley of the valley about 1930, when the donor received its sole use.

L 34¼ in/87 cm; Head H 3¾ in/9.5 cm, W 5 in/ 12.7 cm (NMHT-CL 1980.0338.01). J/G B

115. J B IRON

One such brand was recorded by James Byrnes of Winnemucca in 1874; in 1902 it went to Elko. A similar iron was used by Harvey and then Boggio. This iron was made about 1935 by valley blacksmith Riley.

L (broken) 19 in/48.3 cm; Head H 4 in/10.1 cm, W 5 in/12.7 cm (NMHT-CL 1980.0338.02). J/G B

116. 96 IRON

The brand was recorded in 1914 by the William Stock Farming Co. of Paradise Valley and used by Stock's grandson, Leslie Stewart, owner of the 96 Ranch. This iron was made about 1975 with a perforated pipe handle to reduce heat flow.

Handle L 36 in/91.5 cm; Head H 2⅞ in/7.3 cm, W 5¼ in/13.3 cm. IIM

Bits and Spurs

117. MILLER AND TIETJEN CATALOGUE

Printed for the Reno outlet about 1950, it served buckaroo Leonard Faupel as a source of supply and design for his hand-made bits and spurs.

H 8½in/21.6 cm; W 5 in/12.7 cm (NMHT-CL 1980.0294.21). M/W F (117-137)

118. PAPER SCRAP WITH DESIGN

The design for the cheek plate of a "U.S." type bit resembles several in the catalogue (see item 117).

Design L 7⅛ in/18.1 cm; W 2¼ in/ 5.7 cm (NMHT-CL 1980.0294.01).

119, 120. CARDBOARD PATTERNS

These are patterns for a bit's cheek plate borrowed from numbers 84 and 121 in the catalogue (item 117).

119: L 8¼ in/20.9 cm, W 2¾ in/7 cm. (white); 120: L 8½ in/21.6 cm, W 2⅞ in/7.3 cm (red). (NMHT-CL 1980.0294.02 and 3).

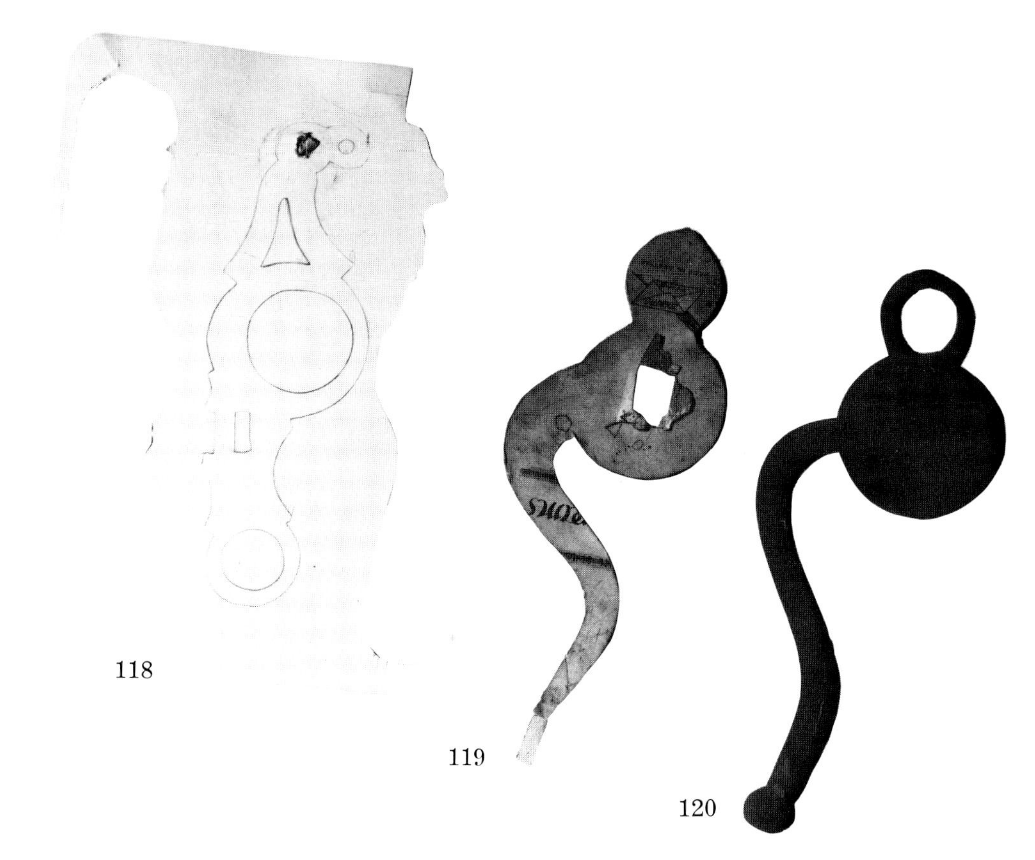

118

119

120

121, 122. METAL PATTERNS

Again, the patterns are for bit cheek plates; one is cut from a tobacco tin, the other from sheet zinc.

121: L 8 15/16 in/22.7 cm, H 2⅞ in/ 7.3 cm; 122: 7⅝ in/19.4 cm, H 3⅜ in/ 8.6 cm (NMHT-CL 1980.0294.04 and 5).

123, 124, 125. METAL PATTERNS

These patterns for "Santa Barbara" bit cheek plates are suggested by numbers 33 and 61 in the Miller and Tietjen catalogue (item 117). Items 123 and 124 are zinc and item 125 is cut from an "M.J.B." coffee tin can.

123: L 6 3/16 in/16.2 cm, H 2 in/5.1 cm; 124: L 7 in/17.8 cm, H 2 1/16 in/5.2 cm; 125: L 8¼ /20.1 cm, H 2 7/16 in/6.2 cm (NMHT-CL 1980.0294.06–8).

117

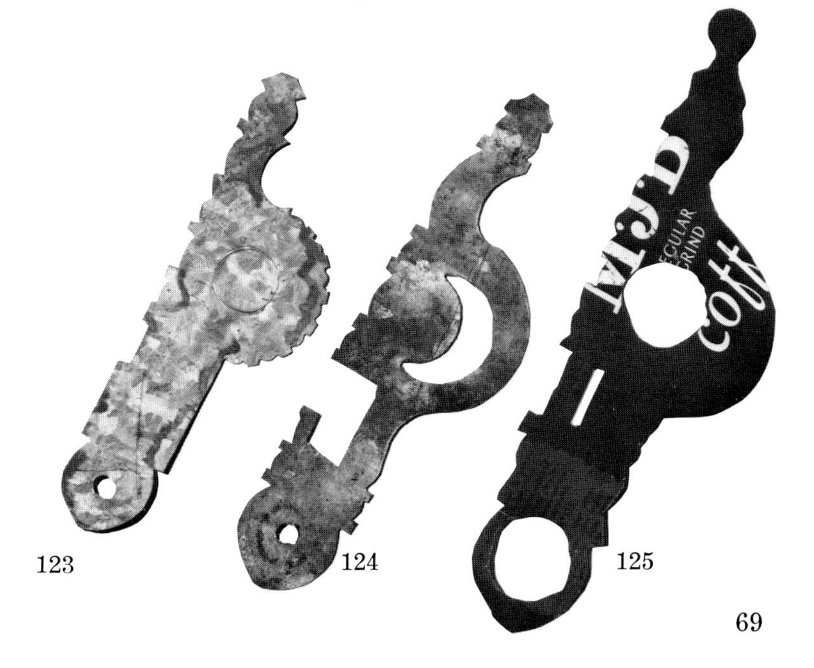

123

124

125

126, 127. CHEEK PLATE BLANKS

These blanks for "Santa Barbara" steel bits reveal areas outlined for silver inlay.

126: L $6\frac{15}{16}$ in/17.6 cm, H $2\frac{1}{8}$ in/5.4 cm; 127: L $7\frac{9}{16}$ in/19.2 cm, H $2\frac{1}{4}$ in/5.8 cm (NMHT-CL 1980.0294.09 and 10).

128. INLAID CHEEK PLATE

The steel blank has inlaid areas of silver.

L $7\frac{9}{16}$ in/19.2 cm; H $2\frac{1}{4}$ in/5.8 cm (NMHT-CL 1980.0294.11).

129. SILVER CHEEK PLATE OVERLAY

The entire part has been cut from a silver sheet and engraved.

L (broken) $6\frac{7}{8}$ in/17.5 cm; H $2\frac{1}{4}$ in/5.7 cm (NMHT-CL 1980.0294.12).

130. ENGRAVED CHEEK PLATE

This steel bit part also reveals silver inlay on the edges of the shank.

L $7\frac{9}{16}$ in/19.2 cm; H $2\frac{3}{8}$ in/6 cm (NMHT-CL 1980.0294.13).

139

131, 132. CHEEK BLANKS WITH STARS

Cut from $\frac{1}{8}$-inch-thick steel, the designs derive from numbers 17 and 19 in the catalogue (item 117).

131: L $8\frac{1}{4}$ in/20.9 cm; H $2\frac{3}{8}$ in/6.1 cm; 132: L 8 in/20.2 cm; H $2\frac{5}{8}$ in/6.7 cm (NMHT-CL 1980.0294.14 and 15).

133, 134. BLANKS FOR SPUR HEEL ARCH

Cut from $\frac{1}{8}$-in-thick steel, these parts make up the heel arch of a spur. Item 133 displays engraved heart inlays in silver and recesses.

133: L $8\frac{7}{16}$ in/21.4 cm, H 1 in/2.5 cm; 134: L $8\frac{1}{2}$ in/21.5 cm, H $1\frac{1}{16}$ in/2.7 cm (NMHT-CL 1980.0294.16 and 17).

135. CHEEK PLATE WITH INLAY

This "Chileno" or ring bit part displays silver inlay on the high arch.

L $5\frac{13}{16}$ in/14.8 cm; H $2\frac{1}{4}$ in/5.7 cm (NMHT-CL 1980.0294.18).

136. CHEEK PLATE BLANK

Made from $\frac{3}{16}$-inch-thick steel plate, the design with inlay recesses appears as number 49 in the catalogue (item 117).

L $7\frac{5}{8}$ in/19.3 cm; H $1\frac{5}{8}$ in/4.1 cm (NMHT-CL 1980.0294.19).

137. CHEEK PLATE BLANK

The "Lady's Leg" design was popular (see item 139) with other buckaroo craftsmen in the region such as Dave Hiller.

L 7 in/17.8 cm; H $1\frac{3}{16}$ in/3.2 cm (NMHT-CL 1980.0294.20).

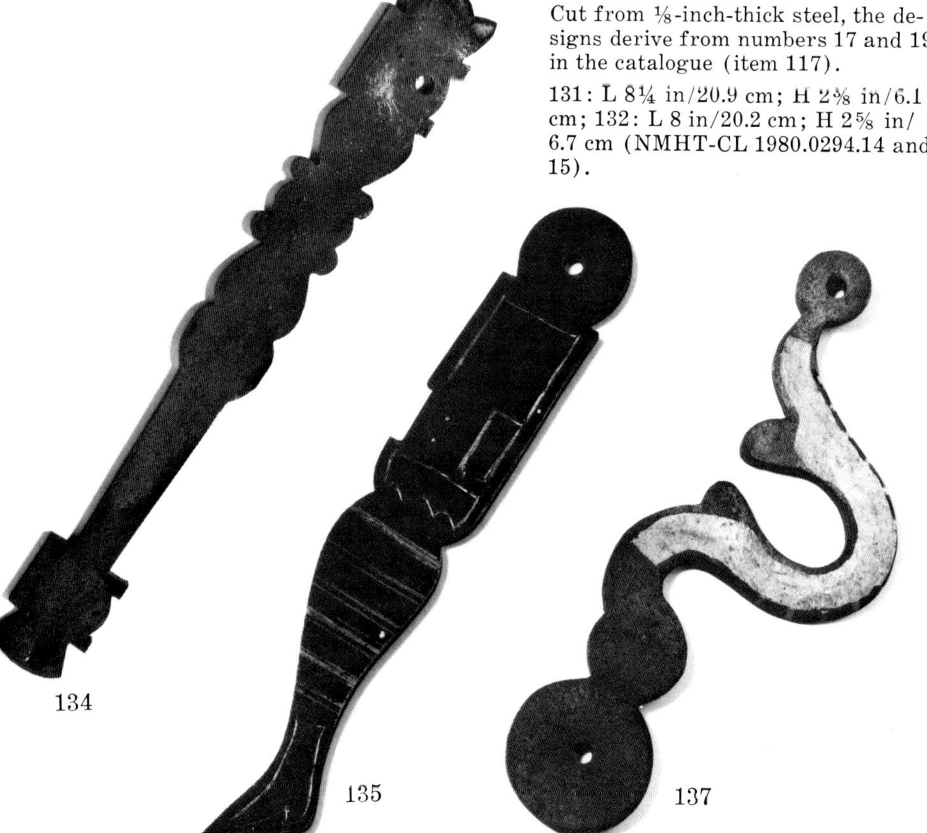

134

135

137

138. BRIDLE WITH CURB BIT

This bridle consists of a headstall, bit, and reins. The leather headstall parts are chin and cheek straps, brow band, and throat latch. The curb bit covered with a copper hood is a "half-breed" type called "Salinas" in a 1980 Garcia catalogue from Elko. The bit is stamped "GARCIA." The steel bit also has engraved silver conchos and a "cricket," or roller, to ease the horse's tongue. The bridle is equipped with flat split reins and a romal, a kind of attached quirt.

Bit L $9\frac{1}{4}$ in/23.2 cm, W $5\frac{7}{8}$ in/14.9 cm; Chain L 10 in/25.4 cm; Reins L 41 in/104.2 cm; Romal L 53 in/134.6 cm; Cheek strap L 39 in/ 99 cm. L/M S

139. SPADE BIT WITH LADY'S LEG

This steel bit cost eighteen dollars when it was bought about 1925 from the Staunton firm of Winnemucca. Despite the cricket, the spade was harder on the mouth than the curb. Note the silver facing engraved to represent a woman's gartered leg (see item 137).

L. $8\frac{3}{16}$ in/20.8 cm; W 6 in/15.3 cm; cheek H $1\frac{5}{8}$ in/4.1 cm. AM

140. HIGH CURB BIT

This iron bit, marked "BUERMANNS," was so inexpensive in the 1930s that it was called the "dollar and a half."

L $6\frac{9}{16}$ in/17.6 cm; W $5\frac{7}{8}$ in/14.9 cm; H $1\frac{7}{8}$ in/4.8 cm. AM

141. SPURS WITH 10-POINT ROWEL

Bought about 1950 by the lender's uncle, Lawrence Paul Miller, the pair of steel and silver spurs is marked with "LPM" and the iron of the Gerhard Miller ranch, the "rocking chair" (see item 103). The identical pair, priced at forty dollars, is illustrated as number 73 in the Miller and Tietjen catalogue (item 117) from Reno, but this pair is marked "Miller & Tietjen/S.F. CAL." The carved stirrup straps vary from the catalogue but are commercial products.

L $6\frac{1}{4}$ in/15.9 cm; W $4\frac{5}{8}$ in/11.7 cm; H $2\frac{1}{8}$ in/5.4 cm; Rowel Diam 2 in/5.1 cm. AM

142. SPURS WITH 14-POINT ROWEL

By the late 1920s, the lender's father, Gerhard Miller, Jr., had bought this iron pair from the firm marked on them, "S(TAUNTON) CO./WINNEMUCCA/NEV." The shank reveals lingering design influences from Hispanic Mexico: the rowel terminal was once a pomegranate motif and the curved post finial, now called a "chap guard," often used an animal motif.

L $6\frac{5}{16}$ in/16 cm; W $4\frac{1}{2}$ in/11.4 cm; H $1\frac{3}{4}$ in/ 4.5 cm; Rowel Diam $2\frac{5}{8}$ in/6.6 cm. AM

143. SPURS WITH SMALL ROWEL

Locally acquired by the lender, the English-type hunting spur, also modified to military use, was used by some buckaroos. This example with a brass rowel is stamped "ROY" and probably dates about 1960.

L 5 in/12.7 cm; W $3\frac{5}{8}$ in/9.2 cm; H $\frac{7}{8}$ in/2.2 cm; Rowel Diam $\frac{7}{8}$ in/2.2 cm. HM

141

Sheep Shearing

Although sheep shearing is not a popular way to earn a living for buckaroos, some signed on for the spring shearing, which included gathering the sheep into pens, dipping, shearing, stamping, and counting them, and sacking their fleece. Paradise Valley no longer has large flocks.

144. SHEARS

Iron shears with spring handles were used to shear sheep and to cut leather and horsehair for craft work. The shears are marked "CAMPBELL [over crown] . . . MADE IN ENGLAND." Many others found in Nevada are marked from Sheffield.

L 13⅜ in/34 cm; Handle W 3¼ in/8.3 cm, D 1 7/16 in/3.6 cm. L/M S

147

144

145. SHEPHERD'S CROOK

The iron rod head dates from about 1930; the ten-foot handle is a replacement. The device was used to catch sheep by the rear leg and also to prod them.

Head L 11 in/28 cm, W 3 in/7.6 cm. PP

146. REVERSE P'S STAMP

According to the lender, this iron rod device was used by Gill Predia about 1915 and later by the Siard outfit to stamp the shorn backs of sheep with paint.

L 11⅛ in/28.2 cm; Head H 5½ in/14 cm, W 4⅝ in/11.7 cm. J/G B

147. H SHEEP STAMP

Carved from pine about 1930 for the local James R. Harvey Co., this device was used, like item 146, to stamp the owner's mark in paint on the backs of shorn sheep.

L 5¾ in/14.6 cm; H and W 3⅞ in/9.8 cm. J/G B

148. H SHEEP IRON

This small, well-made iron of about 1930 branded the owner's mark onto the jaw or horn of sheep.

L 17¾ in/45.1 cm; Head H 13/16 in/2 cm, W ⅝ in/1.6 cm. J/G B

149. J SHEEP IRON

Like item 148, the iron was used to brand sheep horns or jaws with the mark of the owner, John G. Taylor.

L 19½ in/49.5 cm; Head H 2 in/5.1 cm, W 1⅛ in/2.8 cm. J/G B

One-of-A-Kind

150. DITTY BAG

Made about 1960 from the top of an Acme boot, this handy pouch for personal items could be hung from the saddle or a bunkhouse nail.

L 9¾ in/24.8 cm; W 7⅛ in/18.1 cm; Strap L 6½ in/16.5 cm. HM

151. DITTY BAG

Made about 1965 from a blue denim trouser leg, this bag for small items was carried behind the saddle.

L 19¾ in/50.2 cm; mouth W 10¼ in/26 cm. L/M S

150

152

155. FIADOR

Frank Loveland made up this device from a halter with a braided, rawhide hackamore, a twisted cotton rope, and a hair rope or macardy. The last makes a pair of closed reins and a lead or tie line.

Hackamore H 14 in/35.6 cm, L 19 in/ 48.3 cm; Line L 120 in/3.05 m. AM

156. ASHTRAY HOLDER

A local buckaroo-made device from a hame and four "Diamond Hot Forged" horseshoes about 1970. Horseshoes are also used by local blacksmiths to make ranch house gates and gate hooks.

H 24½ in/62.2 cm; Base L 10½ in/ 26.7 cm, W 10 in/25.4 cm (NMHT-CL 1980.0311.02). W/I F

157. COFFEE CAN MOUSE TRAP

This balance-type trap was made from a can marked "Hills Bros Coffee/20 lbs." by Leslie Stewart for the exhibition. Similar ones have long been used in ranch bunkhouses. Half-filled with water, they usually sit at the end of a bench.

H 13¼ in/33.6 cm; W and D 9½ in/ 24.1 cm (NMHT-CL 1980.0292.04).

152. LOW STOOL

Tony Garcia, an itinerant Mexican *vaquero* (buckaroo), made this stool about 1935 on a Paradise Valley ranch. It differs from stools made by Anglo buckaroos in its concave seat of laced thongs and its short, chamfered legs. It has been repainted more than once.

H 13¾ in/34.9 cm; L 18¾ in/47.7 cm; D 15¾ in/40 cm (NMHT-CL 1980.0295.01). DZ

153. HIGH STOOL

Buckaroo Wayne "Lupey" Heller made this stool about 1945. Note the splayed legs and deep skirts under the seat with rounded corners.

H 20⅝ in/52.4 cm; Seat W 14 in/35.6 cm, D 12 in/30.5 cm (NMHT-CL 1980.0311.03). W/I F

154. WORK STOOL

Used on the Boggio ranch since about 1960, the stool shows unusual design in the five-sided legs and their lateral attachment to a long block projecting below the covered seat. It is stable, comfortable, and light.

H 21⅜ in/54.3 cm; Seat W 12⅛ in/ 30.8 cm, D 11 in/28 cm. J/G B

153

157

OVERLEAF:

Les Stewart and Chuck Wheelock, the 96 Ranch.

Bunkhouse

Most ranches have a special separate building called a bunkhouse, where several buckaroos can sleep, stash their few belongings, wash and shave, relax, and even cook and eat. Buildings erected on the grazing range are called line camp cabins and are often a single room for the same daily activities. Objects needed for each activity are efficiently grouped in the room.

158. RECANZONE/SCHNEIDER BUNKHOUSE

This frame building of "single-wall construction" was made about 1920 on the Recanzones' Mill Ranch from wood and composition board. It was built for a respected hand, "Coyote John" Schneider, an itinerant German trapper. It was moved later and served as a storage shed in the corner of a horse corral until Robert Cassinelli sold it to the Smithsonian. This single room provides specific spaces for storing clothing and gear, a bunkbed, and furniture for cooking, eating, cleaning up, and relaxing.

Exterior: L 12 ft 4 in/4.5 m; D 10 ft 2 in/3.7 m; H 10 ft 8 in/3.9 m (NMHT-CL 1980.0293.01).

159. "CAT" HAT

Polyester cap made for the 96 Ranch of Les Stewart. The term "cat" derives from the Caterpillar Company, whose "Diesel Power" slogan adorns a popular version of this baseball-style hat.

H 5 in/12.7 cm; L with bill, 9¾ in/24.8 cm. HM

160. TAN HAT

This rancher's felt "Resistol," bought about 1975, display plastic thongs along the crown creases.

H 6 in/15.2 cm; Brim W 3 in/7.6 cm. L/M S

161. BLACK HAT

This felt hat displays a narrow, buckled belt around the crown. It dates from about 1960.

H 4½ in/11.4 cm; Brim W 3½ in/8.9 cm. PP

162. BROWN HAT

This "Nutria Quality Stetson," entitled "The Nevadan," was sold at Parker's in Reno about 1960. It is marked with the lender's initials, "MP."

H 4¾ in/12.1 cm; Brim W 3 in/7.6 cm. PP

163. JEAN JACKET

Also called a "jumper," this typical blue cotton denim jacket was made by the originating firm of "Levi Strauss & Co./San Francisco/Calif./#70505-0217/Size 46" (copper buttons, leather label), about 1970. It is marked with the lender's initials, "LJS."

L 23 3/16 in/50.9 cm; Underarm W 23¼ in/50.9 cm. L/M S

164. NECKERCHIEF

Also known as a "scarf," "wild rag," or by other names, this black silk piece is well worn after fifteen years of ranch use.

L and W 28 in/71.1 cm. L/M S

160

162

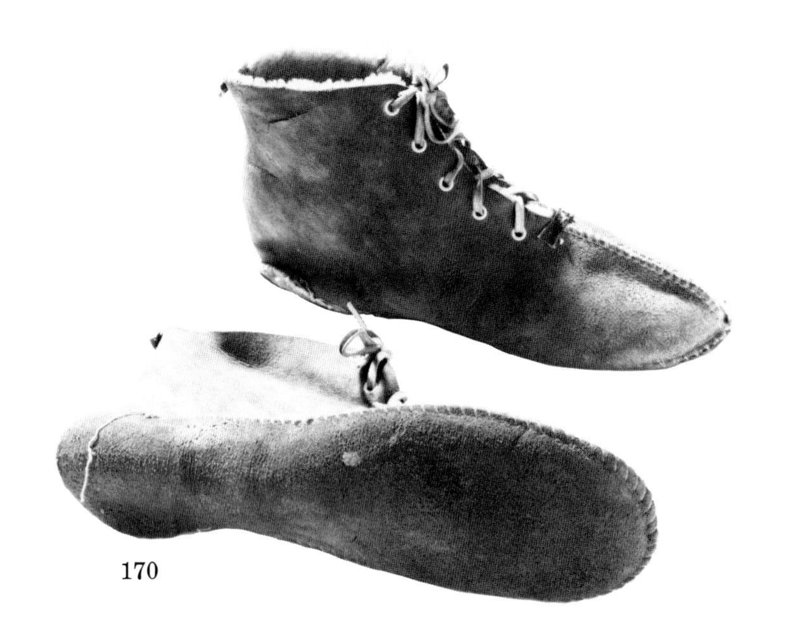

170

165. YELLOW "SLICKER"

This short, heavy raincoat was made with rubberized cloth and closed with snaps; about 1965. The color made the rider more visible.

Back L 30 in/76.2 cm; Sleeve L 23 in/ 58.4 cm; Shoulder W 18 in/45.7 cm; Underarm W 22 in/55.9 cm. L/M S

166. BLACK "SLICKER"

This full-length raincoat of rubberized cloth closed with hinged hooks dates to about 1955.

Back L 48 in/122 cm; Underarm W 24 in/61 cm. PP

167. MUFFLER

This commercial wool plaid scarf dates to about 1950.

L 68 in/172.7 cm; W 14 in/35.6 cm. PP

168. SWEATER

This button-front, navy-blue "Sportswear" was bought by the lender about 1960.

Back H 29 in/73.6 cm; Sleeve L 22 in/ 55.9 cm; Shoulder W 19 in/48.3 cm. PP

169. LINED GLOVES

Bought about 1960, these pigskin gloves are provided with machine-knitted wool liners.

L 13 in/33 cm; W 4½ in/11.4 cm. PP

170. OVERSHOE LINERS

These sheepskin inner shoes were said to be locally made about 1950.

L 10½ in/26.7 cm; H 4½ in/11.4 cm; W 3 in/7.6 cm. PP

171

171. COWBOY BOOTS

This typical western riding boot was made about 1960. Note the decorative stitching and undercut heel employed by the manufacturer, "Leddy/Fort Worth, Texas."

H 12¼ in/31.1 cm; L 11½ in/29.2 cm; W 4⅜ in/11.1 cm. PP

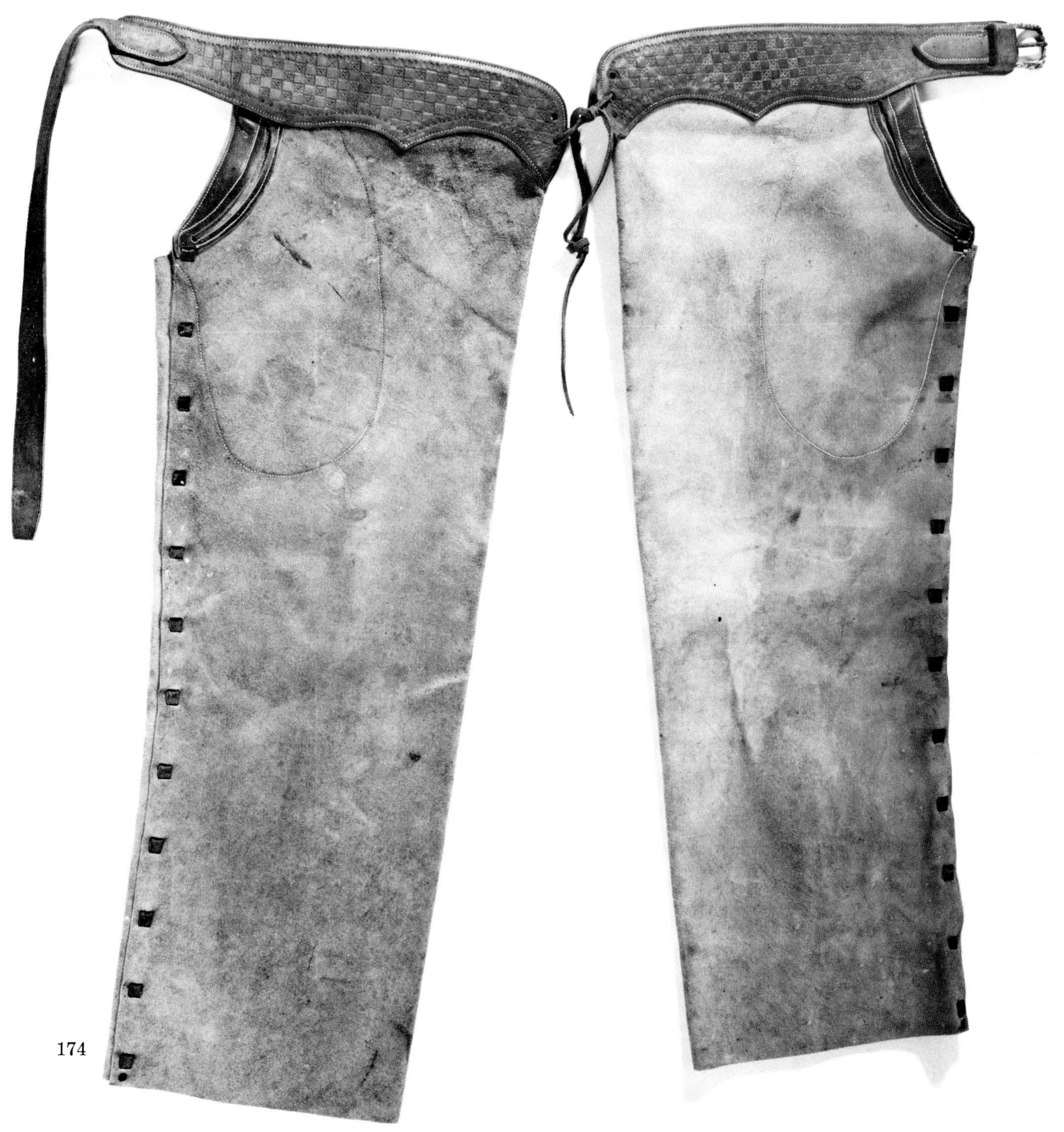

174

172. TROUSERS OR JEANS

These "blue jeans" were made by "Blue Bell Wrangler" from cotton denim with copper buttons, about 1957.

Inseam L 30 in/76.2 cm; Waist 37 in/94 cm. PP

173. HAIR CHAPS

Chaps comes from the Hispanic Mexican word for a rider's leather leg coverings, *las chaparreras*. The pair of Angora goat hide chaps was made about 1935, when hair chaps (or "woolies") began to be replaced by hairless, wider "batwing" and "chinks" types.

L 37 in/94 cm; Leg W 10½ in/26.7 cm. RC

174. SHOTGUN CHAPS

This narrow type of chaps was made about 1945 by "WALT GOLDSMITH/ SADDLERS S.F. CAL." and used by the lender's father, George Miller. Note the set-in pockets.

L 39 in/99 cm/Leg W 14 in/35.6 cm. FM

176

175. SHORT CHAPS OR "CHINKS"

Perhaps a design based on work aprons, this shorter leg protector was developed by buckaroos for work in the corral, on and off horseback. This well-used pair was found on the Garvey Ranch by saddlemaker John Herron.

L 30¾ in/78.1 cm; Leg W 20⅞ in/ 53 cm (NMHT-CL 1979.0252.1).

176. CHINKS

Some pairs of chinks, like these from the 96 Ranch, are cut from old pairs of batwing chaps. These chinks were originally a pair of batwings bought from the N. Porter Company in Phoenix, Arizona, and given to Leslie Stewart by his father, Fred B. Stewart, in 1938. Leslie Stewart wore them for about twenty years and they were then used as supplemental gear for hired buckaroos who did not own their own equipment. This pair of batwings changed into being "chinks" over a period of years as different men, like Paiute Indian buckaroos Clifford Northrup and Donald Dave, made gradual changes.

L 29½ in/94.9 cm; Leg W 21¼ in/ 54 cm. HM

177. BACK BRACE

This hand-made leather device with three buckles gave support to the buckaroo's lower back while he was breaking horses.

L 35 in/88.9 cm; W 7½ in/19 cm. PP

Chuck Wheelock

178-184. A BUCKAROO'S OUTFIT

All the clothing on the mannequin in the bunkhouse was worn as an outfit by Chuck Wheelock of Paradise Valley. The long underwear (item 181) was made by Penman's, the shirt (item 180) by Panhandle Slim, the trousers (item 183) by Levi Strauss, and the boots (item 184) by Paul Bond; the hat with the pheasant feather (item 178) was bought at Stockman's store in Winnemucca. There is also a pair of socks (item 182) and a "wild rag" (item 179, also see item 164) to complete the store-bought outfit. A buckaroo added other personal items like a knife, cigarettes, spurs, jacket, and chaps, according to his taste and needs.

(NMHT-CL 1980.0304.01-7)

185. SHEEPSKIN JACKET

This heavy coat, made about 1950, displays the simple, sturdy construction favored by buckaroos for Nevada winters. The type is being replaced by down-filled jackets popularized by outdoorsmen.

L 27⅜ in/61 cm; Underarm W 19½ in/41 cm. PP

Mannequin by Vernon Rickman, Smithsonian Institution 178-184

OVERLEAF:
Chuck Wheelock at the 96 Ranch fall roundup.

Furnishings

186. SAWBUCK

This traditional device for cutting stove and fireplace wood was made as an exhibit prop by Leslie Stewart, who followed a traditional design.

L 45¼ in/115 cm; H 37½ in/95.3 cm; W 33½ in/85.1 cm.

187. WOOD BOX

This wood and tin-reinforced container was big enough to hold cooking and heating wood for a week. It was made on the lender's ranch about 1940 and has been repainted.

L 66½ in/168.9 cm; H 32½ in/82.5 cm; D 20½ in/52.1 cm. L/M S

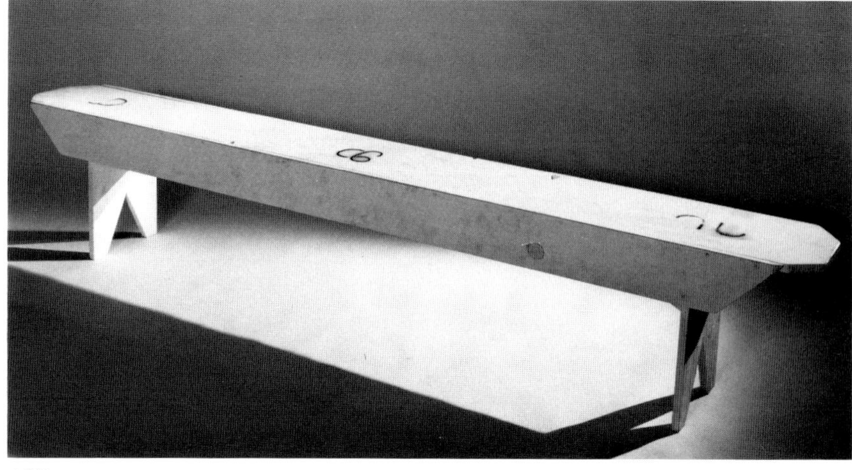

188

188. BENCH

This bunkhouse bench was made by Leslie Stewart for this exhibition and branded with his "96" and other local irons, "JD" and "C6." The form, construction, light color, and use of irons is typical of ranch furniture in the region and derives from a traditional design.

L 96 in/244 cm; H 18 in/45.7 cm; W 12⅞ in/32.7 cm (NMHT-CL 1980.0292.05).

189. DEERSKULL

Such hunting trophies are often mounted on ranch buildings.

W 24 in/61 cm; H 21 in/53.4 cm; D 9 in/22.9 cm. S/M S

190. THERMOMETER

This "Taylor" product dates back to about 1920.

H 9 in/22.9 cm; W 1⅝ in/4.1 cm; D 1¼ in/3.2 cm. J/G B

191. LUCKY HORSESHOE

The shoe is usually placed with the open end up to catch and hold luck.

L and W about 4 in/10.2 cm. J/G B

192. BUNKBED

Built by Leslie Stewart for this exhibition, the bed is space-efficient and inexpensive and follows local preference for light colors in dark bunkhouses. The form derives from a built-in tradition dating back to the Middle Ages. Note the shelf for small personal items.

L 77¾ in/197.3 cm; H 20¾ in/52.7 cm; W 29⅞ in/75.9 cm (NMHT-CL 1980.0292.01).

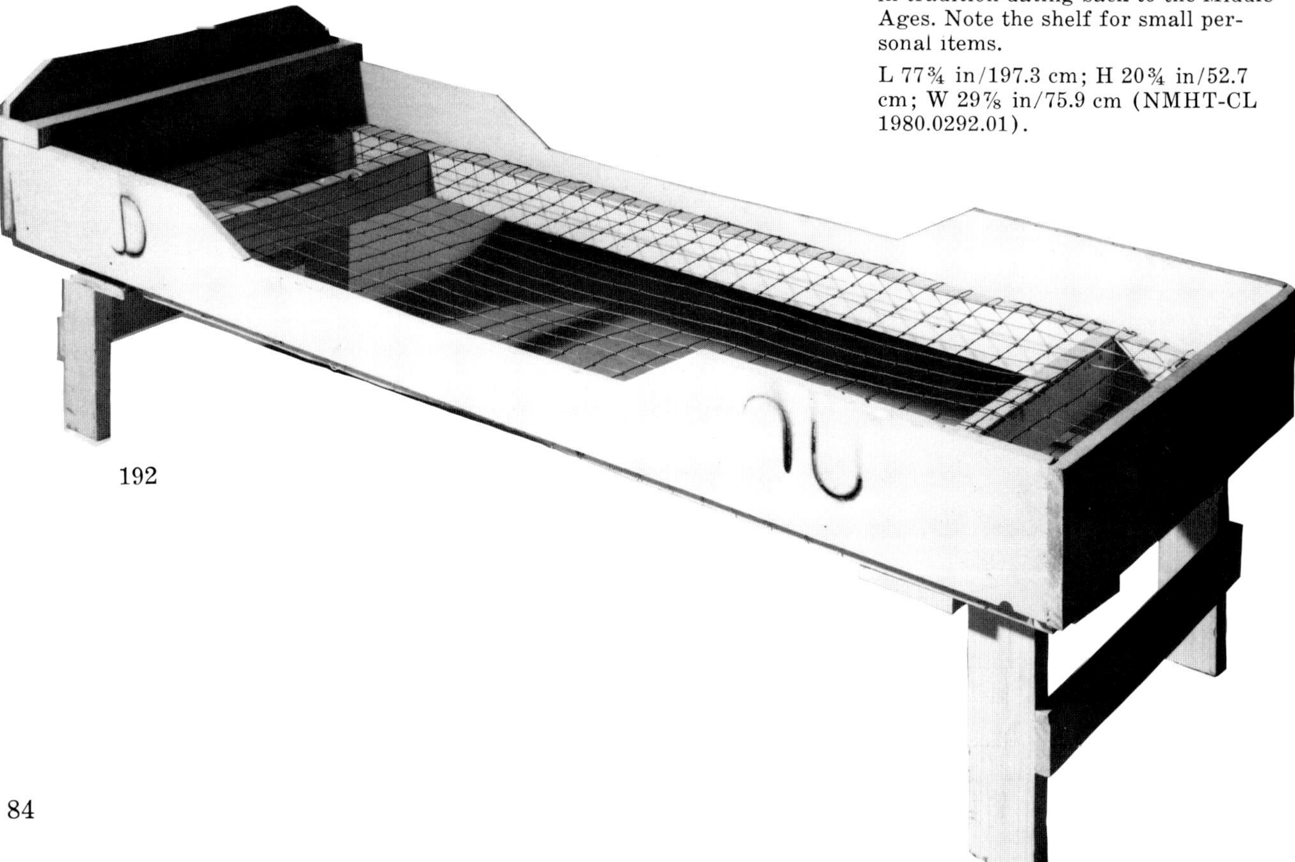

192

193

193, 194. SOUGAN AND COVER

The pieced, cotton quilt or sougan was made about 1935 by the lender's mother, Edith Stock Stewart. It is used on the range or in a bunkbed with a long canvas cover fastened with hooks, a commercial product of the 1960s.

Sougan L 72 in/182.9 cm, W 68 in/172.7 cm; Cover L 197 in/500.4 cm, W 80 in/203.2 cm. L/M S

195, 196. SHELVES

Made by Leslie Stewart for this exhibition, the shelves retain the simple form, light color and built-in practicality of other bunkhouse furniture.

Ls 24 in and 36 in/61 and 91.5 cm; Ds 7¼ in/18.4 cm; H 6¼ in and 7¾ in/16.5 and 19.7 cm (NMHT-CL 1980.0292.02 and 3).

197

197. SIDE CHAIR

Made about 1940 for the Bradshaw line camp cabin, the chair is marked with initials "EB" for Ed Brush and the "TNT" of the Loui Cerri ranch. The plank construction is a modern, western variation of a traditional European type.

H 32¾ in/83.2 cm; Floor-to-seat H 18¾ in/47.6 cm; Seat W 18 in/45.7 cm, D 15½ in/39.4 cm. L/M S

198. KITCHEN TABLE

Like item 187, the pine table was used in the Bradshaw cabin since about 1950. The traditional form with canted corners is covered with oilcloth. The molded-strip drawer has a leather handle and rests on side runners. It is branded with the Stewart ranch "96."

H 31¼ in/79.4 cm; L 72 in/182.9 cm; D 29¼ in/74.3 cm; Drawer W 15 in/38.1 cm; H 3¾ in/9.5 cm, D 19¾ in/50.2 cm. L/M S

199, 200. WAR BAG AND POUCH

Buckaroos also call this a "war sack" and use it to carry their clothing and personal gear. It is a smaller version of the common duffle bag. Items for shaving and washing go in the tan fold-over pouch. The bag bears the Stewart mark, "96."

Bag L 18 in/45.7 cm, Diam 15 in/38.1 cm; Pouch L 13 in/33 cm, folded H 9 in/22.9 cm. L/M S

201. KEROSENE LANTERN

This "PAULL'S" lantern of about 1950 was common to ranch houses and bunkhouses, even after electricity was available.

H 14 in/35.6 cm; Diam 7 in/17.8 cm. PP

204. SHAVING STAND

In time, this elegant device, produced about 1930, might be relegated from the ranch house to the bunkhouse. The glass held soap and the open loop held the lather brush needed to shave with a folding straight-edge razor.

H 13¼ in/33.7 cm; Base Diam 6½ in/16.5 cm. L/M S

205. RAZOR STROP

The "Arabian Shell Winchester" strop, made about 1940, was used to sharpen straight-edge razors.

L 26 in/66 cm; W 2½ in/6.4 cm. PP

206. HAIR TRIMMER

The steel hand trimmer was manufactured as "PRIEST'S BOUDOIR" about 1940. It provided the buckaroo with the closest thing to a "shop cut."

L 5 in/12.7 cm; H 3⅝ in/9.2 cm; Head W 1½ in/3.8 cm. J/G B

207, 208. WASH BASIN AND PITCHER

This set of white enameled ironware served for a wash-up and shave.

Basin: H 3½ in/8.9 cm, Diam 12½ in/31.8 cm; Pitcher: H 9 in/22.9 cm, Spout-to-handle W 9¾ in/24.8 cm. L/M S

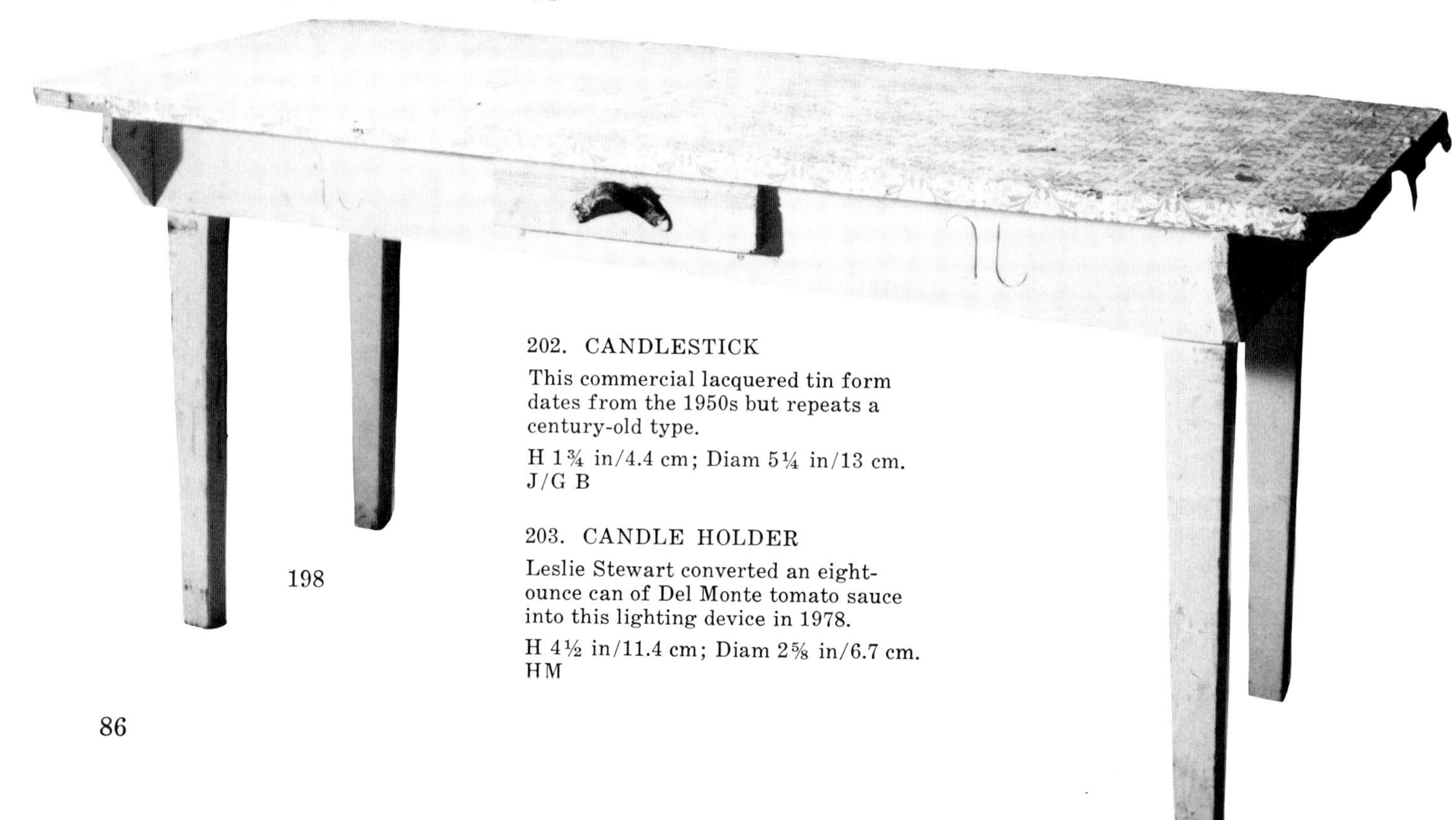

198

202. CANDLESTICK

This commercial lacquered tin form dates from the 1950s but repeats a century-old type.

H 1¾ in/4.4 cm; Diam 5¼ in/13 cm. J/G B

203. CANDLE HOLDER

Leslie Stewart converted an eight-ounce can of Del Monte tomato sauce into this lighting device in 1978.

H 4½ in/11.4 cm; Diam 2⅝ in/6.7 cm. HM

Dave Hiller at the Circle A Little Owyhee line camp.

209

209. FIRST-AID KIT

Marked "BOYT 8-43," the kit contains bandages, salves, and a snakebite device.

L 5 in/12.7 cm; H 3½ in/8.9 cm; D 2 in/5.1 cm. L/M S

210

Reading Material

210-212. MAGAZINES AND BOOKS

Old magazines like *Reader's Digest* (1942) and pocket books like Norman's *Oklahoma Crude* (1973) and Vernadsky's *History of Russia* (1962), both used by buckaroo Herb Pembroke, helped pass time in the bunkhouse.

Digest: H 7½ in/19 cm; W 5¼ in/13.3 cm; *Crude* and *Russia:* H 7 in/17.8 cm; W 4¼ in/10.8 cm. J/G B, HM

213. COAL AND WOOD BURNING STOVE

This compact stove is marked "(MA?) C STOVE & RANGE CO./SHEFFIELD ALA./" and bears a raised "M over S & R Co" emblem. It served for cooking and heating. About 1940.

H 28 in/71.1 cm; W 23¼ in/59.1 cm; L 34½ in/87.6 cm. PP

214. GRIDDLE

This factory iron casting of about 1960 served both indoors and out.

L 21 in/53.4 cm; W 9 in/22.9 cm. PP

216

213

215. FRY PAN

This skillet is a factory iron casting of about 1950. It is marked only "5X."

H 1¾ in/4.4 cm; Diam 8 in/20.3 cm. PP

216. FRY PAN

This rolled-tin skillet is marked "COLD HANDLE/ACME N.Y. STAMPING CO./ BROOKLYN USA," and dates about 1950. The long, hollow handle helps prevent burned hands.

L 13 in/33 cm; H 2 in/5.1 cm. PP

217. STEW POT

This iron casting of about 1940 cooked up all kinds of meals, including "son-of-a-gun stew."

H 4 in/10.2 cm; Diam 10 in/25.4 cm. PP

218. SAUCE PAN

This "WEAR EVER" model was cast about 1950 in aluminum.

H 4 in/10.2 cm; Diam 6¼ in/10.8 cm. PP

219. COFFEE POT

This twelve-cup rolled aluminum pot of about 1950 repeats a century-old type familiar in the West. Note the thread spool finial.

H 10 in/25.4 cm; Diam 6 in/15.3 cm. L/M S

217

219

220, 221. ENAMELWARE PLATES

These gray and white enameled iron-ware plates date from about 1950. The white one (item 220) is marked "K.E.R. SWEDEN, 24 cms." Both are common on Nevada ranches.

Hs 1 in/2.5 cm; Diam 9 in and 9½ in/ 22.9 cm and 24.1 cm. L/M S

222. EARTHENWARE SAUCER

This commercial glazed ware from the Stewart ranch was made about 1930 and is marked "Buffalo China."

H ¾ in/1.9 cm; Diam 5⅞ in/14.9 cm. L/M S

223-225. WOODEN-HANDLED UTENSILS

The four-tine fork and dinner knife with three brass rivets and the darker, three-tine fork with two brass rivets are typical of ranch utensils in the period from 1880 to 1930.

Fork 223: 7 3/16 in/18.2 cm, W ⅞ in/ 2.3 cm; Knife: 8¾ in/22.2 cm, W 13/16 in/2.1 cm; Fork 225: L 7½ in/9.1 cm, W 11/16 in/1.7 cm. L/M S

223-225

226-232. METAL UTENSILS

A variety of stamped and rolled white metal utensils were available at reasonable cost. These date from 1910 to 1940. Spoon 226 is marked "WB" over "W/STAINLESS STEEL"; fork 227 is marked "W.M. SILVER PLATE"; the second fork 228 bears "W R" with two marks; the three tine fork 229 is unmarked; the third fork 230 is stamped "900" over "WB" over "W" and "MADE IN USA"; knife 231 bears only "STAINLESS U.S.A."; and knife 232 is unmarked.

Spoon 226: L 8⅛ in/20.6 cm, W 1¾ in/4.5 cm; Fork 227: L 7⅛ in/18 cm, W 1 in/2.5 cm; Fork 228: L 7¼ in/18.5 cm, W 1 in/2.5 cm; Fork 229: L 7³⁄₁₆ in/18.2 cm, W ¹¹⁄₁₆ in/1.7 cm; Fork 230: L 7¼ in/18.5 cm, W¹⁵⁄₁₆ in/2.4 cm; Knife 231: L 8¹³⁄₁₆/22.4 cm, W ⅝ in/1.6 cm; Knife 232: L 9⁵⁄₁₆ in/23.6 cm, W ⅞ in/2.2 cm. L/M S

236

233. BUTCHER KNIFE

This factory product of wood, steel, and brass dates about 1950. It is carved with the ranch iron "96."

L 9 in/22.9 cm; W 1⅛ in/2.8 cm. L/M S

234. UTENSIL BOX

This pine box was made by hand, probably on the Stewart ranch about 1950.

H 7 in/17.8 cm; L 10 in/25.4 cm; D 5½ in/14 cm. L/M S

235, 236, 237. ENAMELED CUPS

Two white (items 235, 236) and one gray (item 237) ironware cups suggest the narrow range of color and form available. One (item 236) was used for target practice.

Hs 2½ in, 3 in, 3 in/6.3 cm, 7.6 cm; Diams 4 in/10 cm (236: NMHT-DL 1980.0036.01). L/M S, PP

238, 239. SUGAR BOWL AND CREAM PITCHER

These commercial pressed-glass products date from about 1940.

Bowl: H 5½ in/14 cm, W 4¼ in/10.8 cm; Pitcher: H 4⅛ in/10.5 cm, W 4½ in/11.4 cm. J/G B

240. SALT SHAKER

The molded glass body is marked "B" in a circle, and the celluloid lid, "MACDONALD & GEHM N.Y.C.," products of the 1950s.

H 4 in/10.2 cm; Base W 2¾ in/7 cm. J/G B

241. STIRRING PADDLE

This factory product of oak was made about 1950.

L 19 in/48.3 cm; W 2 in/5.1 cm. J/G B

242. CORKSCREW

This item was manufactured about 1950.

L 3¼ in/8.2 cm; W 3 in/7.6 cm. J/G B

243. ENAMELED PAN

Gray ironware cooking utensils have been common on ranches since the 1880s; this pan dates about 1940.

H 2 in/5.1 cm; Diam 11⅛ in/28.2 cm (NMHT-DL 1979.0254.5).

244. U-GRILLE

Made about 1960 from an iron rod, this device was easily stored and transported, often in a bag behind the saddle cantle.

L 20 in/50.8 cm; W 5 in/12.7 cm. PP

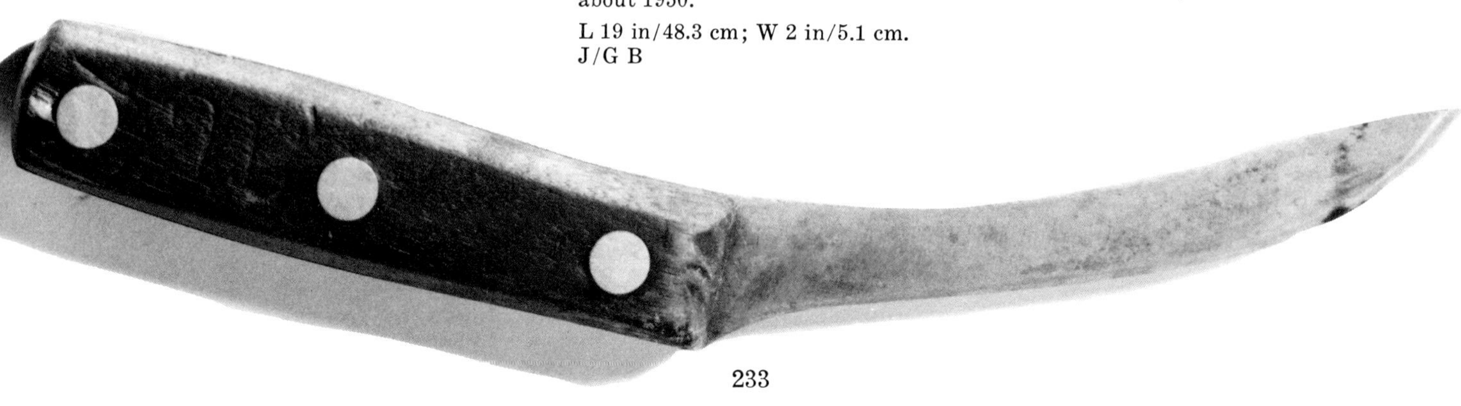
233

Dan Martinez

Bob Humphrey and Clale Northrup, the 96 Ranch.

Selected Readings

Adams, Andy. *The Log of a Cowboy: A Narrative of the Old Trail Days.* Lincoln: University of Nebraska Press, 1964.

Adams, Ramon F. *Come An' Get It: The Story of the Old Cowboy Cook.* Norman: University of Oklahoma Press, 1953.

Adams, Ramon F. *The Cowman and His Philosophy.* Austin: Encino Press, 1967.

Ahlborn, Richard E. *Early Saddles of Western North America.* Washington: Smithsonian Institution Press, 1980.

Angel, Myron (ed.). *History of Nevada with Illustrations and Biographical Sketches of Its Prominent Men and Pioneers.* 1881. Reprint. Berkeley: Howell-North Books, 1958.

Back, Joe. *Horse, Hitches and Rocky Trails.* Chicago: Sage Books, Swallow Press, 1959.

Beitz, Les. *Treasury of Frontier Relics, a Collector's Guide.* New York: Edwin House, 1966.

Bragg, Allen C. *Humboldt County, 1905* Winnemucca: North Central Nevada Historical Society, 1976.

Branch, Douglas. *The Cowboy and His Interpreters.* New York: D. Appleton and Company, 1926.

Carlson, Helen. *Nevada Place Names: A Geographical Dictionary.* Reno: University of Nevada Press, 1974.

Clawson, Marion. *The Western Range Livestock Industry.* New York: McGraw-Hill, 1950.

Clifton, Robert T. *Barbs, Prongs, Points, Prickers and Stickers, A Complete and Illustrated Catalog of Antique Barbed Wire.* Norman: University of Oklahoma Press, 1970.

Dobie, J. Frank. *The Longhorns.* Boston: Little, Brown and Company, 1941.

Elliott, Russell B. *History of Nevada.* Lincoln: University of Nebraska Press, 1973.

Elliott, Russell B. and Helen J. Poulton. *Writings on Nevada: A Selected Bibliography.* Carson City: University of Nevada Press, 1963.

Frantz, Joe B., and Julian Ernest Choate, Jr. *The American Cowboy: The Myth and the Reality.* Norman: University of Oklahoma Press, 1955.

Hulse, James W. *The Nevada Adventure: A History.* Reno: University of Nevada Press, 1972.

James, Will. *Cowboys North and South.*
New York: Charles Scribner's Sons, 1924.

Jones, Mrs. Adell (Casey). "An April Visit to Paradise Valley." *Nevada Highways and Parks* 16:2 (1956), 3-13.

Laxalt, Robert. *Nevada: A Bicentennial History.*
New York: W. W. Norton Company, 1977.

McDowell, Bart. *The American Cowboy in Life and Legend.*
Washington: National Geographic Society, 1972.

Mora, Jo. *Trail Dust and Saddle Leather.*
New York: Charles Scribner's Sons, 1946.

Mora, Jo. *Californios.*
Garden City, N.Y.: Doubleday and Company, 1949.

Olson, Debbie Stewart. "An Early Pioneer in Paradise Valley." *Official Nevada Day Magazine* (Carson City, 1965), 24-28.

Osgood, Ernest Staples. *The Day of the Cattleman.*
1929. Reprint. Chicago: University of Chicago Press, 1966.

Rojas, Arnold J. *The Vaquero.*
Charlotte, Santa Barbara, Calif.: McNally and Loftin, 1964.

Rollins, Philip Ashton. *The Cowboy: His Characteristics, His Equipment, and His Part in the Development of the West.*
New York: Charles Scribner's Sons, 1922.

Savage, William W. *Cowboy Life: Reconstructing an American Myth.*
Norman: University of Oklahoma Press, 1975.

Shepperson, Wilbur S. *Restless Strangers: Nevada's Immigrants and Their Interpreters.*
Reno: University of Nevada Press, 1970.

State of Nevada, Department of Agriculture. *Official Livestock Brand Book, 1976.*
Reno: State of Nevada, 1976.

Thompson and West's history of Nevada (see Angel, Myron (ed.). *History of Nevada).*

Thorp, N. Howard ("Jack"). *Songs of the Cowboys.*
New York: Bramhall House, 1956.

Truett, Velma Stevens. *On the Hoof in Nevada.*
Los Angeles: Cehret-Truett-Hall, 1950.

Western States Historical Publishers, Inc. *Nevada, the Silver State.*
Carson City: Western States Historical Publishers, 1970.

Wheat, Margaret M. *Survival Arts of the Primitive Paiutes.*
Reno: University of Nevada Press, 1967.

Works Progress Administration, Nevada Writers Project. *Nevada: A Guide to the Silver State.*
Portland, Oregon: Binfords, 1940.

Photograph Credits

The following list identifies the photographers and provides the negative numbers for the photographs taken in Nevada. All of these pictures, or copies of pictures in the case of historic photographs, are part of the collection created at the Library of Congress by the Paradise Valley Folklife Project. Photographers for the project whose photographs appear in this book are Carl Fleischhauer, Suzi Jones, Howard W. Marshall, William Smock, and William A. Wilson.

All of the studio photographs of artifacts from the exhibition were made by Alfred Harrell of the Office of Printing and Photographic Services, Smithsonian Institution.

Cover. Fleischhauer (NV 6-19754-19)
ii-iii. Fleischhauer (NV 4367-33)
iv. Marshall (NV 31-20656-8)
vii. Fleischhauer (NV 156704-9-25A)
xii. Leslie Stewart by Fleischhauer (NV 156770-9-20A)
xii. Marie Stewart by Marshall (NV 5-19413-18A)
xiii. Geraldine and Joe Boggio by Smock (NV 4672-36)
xiii. Fred Miller by Fleischhauer (NV 4592-1)
xiii. Robert Cassinelli by Marshall (NV 4631-7)
xiv. Walter Fischer by Smock (NV 4668-2)
xiv. Ann Miller by Marshall (NV 156770-12-35)
xiv. Alvin Miller and Wesley Faupel by Smock (NV 4674-8A)
xv. Pete Pedroli by Smock (NV 4937-28)
xv. Delfina Zatica by Jones (NV 9-19966-27)
xv. Marguerite Faupel by Smock (NV 4931-36)

1. Marshall (NV 14-19492-28A)
2. Fleischhauer (NV 4-19387-4)
4. Marshall (NV 35-20656-12A)
5. Courtesy of Fritz Buckingham (NV 4526-14)
8. Courtesy of Joe Boggio (NV 2-19386-9)
9. Fleischhauer (NV 3-19354-10)
10. Courtesy of Leslie and Marie Stewart (NV 4563-11). This picture is exhibition artifact 2.
10-11. Courtesy of Loui Cerri (NV 23739)
13. Fleischhauer (NV 4588-25)
14. Wilson (NV 5-19516-16)
16. Fleischhauer (NV 80-CF8-18) Original in color.
17. Marshall (NV 156890-4-2)
19. Smock (NV 6452-17A)
20. Wilson (NV 3-19462-28)
21. Fleischhauer (NV 4581-24)
22. Fleischhauer (NV 4586-22)
23. Marshall (NV 4658-8)
24. Marshall (NV 2-19515-14)
25. Smock (NV 4668-12)
27. Jones (NV 12-20657-22)
28. Fleischhauer (NV 4365-6A)
29. Marshall (NV 8-20656-30)
30. Marshall (NV 1-19515-12)
32. Fleischhauer (NV 6-19754-29)
34-35. Fleischhauer (NV 4593-8)
37. Marshall (NV 2-19515-30)
39. Ahlborn (NV 20049-22)
40. Marshall (NV 9-19492-6)
41. Marshall (NV 5-19413-26)
42. Fleischhauer (NV 10-19412-7)
43. Marshall (NV 1-19387-24A)
44. Smock (NV 4567-25)
45. Courtesy of Angie Genasci (NV 159160-1-9)
46. Fleischhauer (NV 156704-9-3A)
58-59. Fleischhauer (NV 4361-34)
74-75. Marshall (NV 12-20010-25)
76. Fleischhauer (NV 4686-6)
77. Marshall (NV 2-19515-13A)
80. Marshall (NV 33-20656-11A)
81. Marshall (NV 7-20010-20A)
82-83. Marshall (NV 1-19420-24)
87. Marshall (NV 3-19492-30A)
91. Fleischhauer (NV 24-19754-23)
92. Marshall (NV 27-20656-30)

96 Ranch branding iron.

Designed by Gerard A. Valerio, Bookmark Studio

Composed in Linotype Century Expanded and Trylon
by Service Composition, Baltimore, Maryland

Printed on Warren's Lustro Enamel
by Eastern Press, New Haven, Connecticut